I Used to Say My Mother

was Shirley Bassey

I Used to Say My Mother was Shirley Bassey

Stephen K Amos

Constable • London

Constable & Robinson Ltd
55–56 Russell Square
London WC1B 4HP
www.constablerobinson.com

First published in the UK by Constable,
an imprint of Constable & Robinson Ltd, 2012

A copy of the British Library Cataloguing in
Publication data is available from the British Library

ISBN: 978-1-78033-857-6 (hardback)
ISBN: 978-1-78033-889-7 (ebook)

Printed and bound in the UK

1 3 5 7 9 10 8 6 4 2

Prologue: South London, 1980s

'K-THWACK K-THWACK K-THWACK K-THWACK.'

'Doo doo duh doo duh doo doo duh doo.'

'No I . . . CAN'T wait. No I . . . CAN'T wait, anoTHER MINute! For it all to begin!'

That was Jonny and his wife Natalie, our white neighbours when I lived in Fountain Road in Tooting. It was a three-bedroom flat in one of those red brick 1940s council blocks and, including Mum and Dad, there were seven of us squeezed into it. We hadn't been there long and Dad said he was going to do it up. It needed doing up as there were holes in the kitchen walls, the fuse blew if you turned on the telly and even though it was a ground-floor flat, somehow, the ceiling leaked.

Jonny and Natalie were trying to sing the latest 5 Star song for our general amusement. Something our parents would never have done. Together they sounded terrible. Separately they sounded pretty terrible. But with everyone in the room clapping time along with them? Well, they weren't going to win any big awards but it would do for a Sunday morning. Even Maxine, Natalie's white-haired elderly mother, had come along that day and sat in a chair in the corner guffawing with laughter.

1

In case you don't remember, 5 Star were the short-lived British equivalent to The Jackson 5. By which I mean they were a family of singers, they were black, and their dad used to manage them. My twin sister Stella and I were showing off the moves we'd been learning from watching our favourite band on *Top of the Pops* as everyone else clapped out the beat. We had all the steps down pat. We were two thirteen-year-olds, looking pretty fly, holding out the shoulders of our T-shirts to mimic those massive shoulder pads everyone on TV used to wear.

Jonny and Natalie were of similar age to my parents, and Dad worked with Jonny in construction. They'd helped dispel my parents' mistrust of the area when we'd moved in a few months previously by making us feel very much at home. We really looked forward to them coming round as they were great fun. They had no children of their own and so I wondered where their youthful sense of vitality came from, because my parents couldn't have been more different. Mum and Dad were feeling the pressure because this was the late eighties and we were already a big family living on a tight budget. Growing up we had to share everything – clothes, bedrooms and even bathwater. I was sixteen before I realised that water didn't come out of the tap grey (and hairy). Looking back I'm not surprised my parents were constantly stressed out as it costs so much to raise kids. I read somewhere that by the time a child reaches eighteen you can have spent £100,000. And that's just on Valium.

Jonny and Natalie sometimes came around to babysit us and we were encouraged to call them Uncle and Auntie. This was not unusual as every friend of the family was automatically an auntie or an uncle. Sometimes they didn't even have to be a friend. Even the milkman was an uncle to us. That was until the unfortunate incident when for a laugh I told my youngest sister Cordelia that the milkman had a special udder and that she should go and pull it. I didn't think that she would actually do it. He never came around again and as punishment it became my job to get milk every day from the Happy Shopper down the road. This turned out to be a blessing in disguise because the Indian man who ran the shop would always give me a free Wham! bar to chew on the way home, thus bolstering my already rampant addiction to sweets.

'Where's the party?' Mum poked her head around the door from the sizzling kitchen to look at the front room with Stella and me dancing centre of the makeshift stage. Mum always called it a party at the weekends when all the kids and parents were home at the same time. A more accurate description would be a whirlwind of destruction with an occasional pause for meal breaks. Normally, when Mum said something like 'Where's the party?' it meant you had better shut it up right now or you were going to get thumped into the middle of next week, but at the weekend we cranked the volume up to full blast. It was the Amos family in high fidelity.

Sunday was the best day of the week because the whole family could enjoy a proper cooked breakfast. In time they would become so legendary that half of our neighbours on the block would turn up for a grilled tomato or a slice of ham. With five kids in the family (and another on the way) we had to have cereal every other day of the week and no sugar. Sometimes no milk. I hated cereal so much by the time I was ten years old that I promised myself when I grew up I'd never eat a bowl of it again. The only good thing about cereal was the tiny toy you used to get at the bottom of the box. But it was always the same toy. A bicycle reflector! I had about a hundred of them – all the colours of the rainbow. I didn't let the fact that I had no bike put me off collecting them. I spent most of my school days trying to get someone to buy me a bike. I used to leave Littlewoods catalogues open at the BMX page but

Dad didn't take the hint. When I started pinning half a dozen of my best bicycle reflectors to my school jacket I hoped he'd think I looked sad enough and cave in. But that isn't his style. He said I looked so cool and this way everyone would see me coming a mile away. Well, they could, but I might have looked a bit funny because most of them didn't come any closer.

A voice from the kitchen:

'Where is your father? Jonny, have you sent him out to work on a Sunday? Can't a man have peace just for a day?' Jonny and Dad worked together professionally, but they also used to do local odd jobs in the area to help people out. Sort of like handymen. They could be out at night-time, in the day and even at the weekends. Whenever. Mum couldn't always find Dad (especially if he was hiding from her) but Jonny could. They were best friends.

'Not me. Maybe he's gone to church.' Jonny winked at me.

'At church? He has already found his angel in me, so he can't be there. Unless! Ah! He has found another wife!' Mum came swinging into the living room brandishing a skillet. 'Let me at him. I will go back home to Nigeria for him if he has run away with some wretched woman.'

Mum was still cut-and-thrusting with the frying pan and pulling a mean-looking face when Dad walked right in the front door and almost lost an eye. He smiled his big broad smile. 'Ah! Ifemi! How now?!' He always called her either *ifemi*, which means 'my love' in Yoruba, or simply 'mummy'.

'Why are you smiling? Don't show your teeth like that?! Do you want to eat me?' The thing about Mum and Dad was, I could never tell if they were joking or really arguing. Well, they're still together today so they must have been joking most of the time. That's Nigerian people for you. Sometimes if you walk down the street and see two Nigerians shouting at each other you think they might be about to come to blows but they are really good friends. We come from an expressive culture and that means that my mum could pretty much terrify anyone just by talking to them. Great if you're getting bullied by the local kids for not having the latest trainers, not so great if you're queuing up at the post office to buy a stamp and a little old lady in front is taking too long at the counter.

'What is this racket going on in here? Mummy, the bacon is already in the frying pan so why does it sound like you are killing the pig? Jonny, my friend! How are you, Mr Man? And Natalie here as well?' He kissed her on the cheek. 'Good to see you too Maxine.' Dad would always bow down low when he greeted Maxine, Natalie's mother. It's a big Nigerian thing to pay respect to your elders. If I met my older relatives any time and didn't give them proper respect Dad would give my ears two boxes. In Nigeria it's a regular thing to see grown men fully prostrate themselves in the street when they are greeting older people. It means that saying hello to a big group of seniors can take upwards of half an hour.

I'm pretty sure we were the first black people Maxine had ever spoken to and I think Dad liked to play with her expectations. She always giggled and blushed bright red when Dad greeted her like this, and so every time they met he bowed a little lower and for a little longer. 'Oh stop it!' she'd say in a broad cockney accent. But secretly she loved it as she regularly commented on how much Dad looked like Sydney Poitier – 'You know that dark fella in them films! Oh! If only I was a bit younger!' She was a typical, jolly, old lady with silver hair and a friendly smile. She'd lived in the area since just after World War II when the flats were built.

'Mummy!' Dad embraced my mum, who shooed him away with a greasy spatula. 'Ah, no greeting for your husband?'

'Fine words do not produce food!' But she kissed him anyway before heading back to the kitchen. 'Have you been working?'

'Of course not. Jonny is here and he is the boss. Not to oversee workmen is to leave your purse open.'

Dad laid a hand on Jonny's shoulder, who paused from his 'Doo duh duhs' to look up at Dad and say, 'How did you get on with the Cit–?' My dad glared at him, but before anything else could be said Stella cut in.

'Jonny! You're messing up the beat!' My twin sister was twirling in the middle of the room doing the all-important 5 Star solo section and miming into a hairbrush. Stella is a great singer but Natalie was supplying the vocals today ('My heart is reeeeeaching for you. And my looooooove is getting stronger').

But I'd seen enough to know that Dad was up to something and had been out getting a surprise present for Mum. I knew it would be a disaster at that moment, but I had no idea what kind of disaster it would turn out to be. He often surprised Mum with 'presents'. You see Dad is a serial hoarder. Collecting stamps, coins or even dolls, I understand. I appreciate that different objects mean different things to different people, but there is a fine line between stuff and rubbish. Things any normal person would describe as rubbish. He is the kind of guy who if he drove past a hedge with an old TV in it would stop the car and put the TV in the boot, talking about how he was going to fix it up for the front room. So I knew that he'd have something 'interesting' to give to my mum later on in the day and then we'd have a fun hour of Dad trying to explain to her why an old Amstrad computer system reclaimed from a skip was going to revolutionize the world. The scars must have remained because even today Mum still doesn't use a computer and back then, well, no one did, so it really was a lost cause.

Years later, when I moved out of home, my old bedroom instantly turned into a scene out of *Steptoe and Son*. If you want three broken Betamaxes or an Etch-a-Sketch with a cracked screen, go and see my dad. He just can't throw anything away. Last time I checked there was a box full of hopelessly entangled Slinkies and even a deflated old Spacehopper in there. Remember the Spacehopper? Never has a product promised so much but delivered so little – except for maybe edible underwear, or the Skoda Superb.

At that moment Mum came sailing out of the kitchen with plates and plates of steaming breakfast. The mouth-watering smells of fried bacon, fried sausage, fried egg, crisp fried bread, charred tomato, thick sliced gammon and delicious potato filled the room and everyone went for it with gusto. In the Amos household you had to eat quick unless you wanted your neighbour's poaching fork to spear a tasty morsel.

Mum and Dad worked so much that as a kid I learned to cook from a very young age. I must have been the only ten year-old on the block who knew how to use a deep fat fryer. It was probably quite a dangerous situation, but we're talking about the eighties when health and safety rules didn't apply. To this day food for me is a very important barometer for happiness. I like to sit and have lunch with friends and talk about what we might have for dinner. I like to eat steak and think about what flavour ice cream I can have for dessert. Asking around, I've noticed that anyone who grew up with lots of brothers and sisters has this same attitude. It comes from the regular habit of hungry siblings trying to steal your food.

Contented gurglings gave way to loud slurpings of sweet milky tea as Cordelia, only six years old, gathered the yolk-streaked plates into the kitchen. Already excited by what was to come my dad made his announcement.

'Today is your mother's birthday!' Well, that was news to us. This was the first time I'd ever heard Dad announce a birthday like that. Before you start crying on about what terrible children we were for not knowing it was our own mother's birthday, you have to understand that in the Amos family we were discouraged from making a big fuss or spending good money on any occasion. I can't tell you the amount of Old Spice deodorant gift packs I received for my birthday between the ages of five and eighteen, by which time they deemed me old enough not to receive anything at all. The answer is thirteen. And I think the only reason I got a present was because I was born a twin and so the date was etched on my mum's brain to such an extent that she couldn't forget it. But being a twin meant that my sister and I even had to share presents. It was my school PE teacher who had to come up to me and explain that there really was no such thing as a unisex training bra. I once asked my mum what it was like having twins. She said, 'Ah Stephen! It was all the joy of having one child . . . but totally ruined.'

It wasn't just birthdays that were downplayed. We never did much for Mother's Day or Father's Day and I don't think Mum and Dad even remembered when their wedding anniversary was. I reckon Dad would've been quite happy telling us we were Jehovah's Witnesses if he thought the kids would believe him and let him get away with cancelling Christmas. Mum wasn't very keen on Christmas either because for several years she worked for the postal service and had to spend that cold December morning delivering cards to other people's houses – normally while heavily pregnant. New Years Day would come and go but the only reason we knew anything had happened was because the date changed. Dad's philosophy was simple: if you don't have to go to work or school on a public holiday then that is enough of a reward – there's no need to make a big song and dance over everything. So it was very surprising to us kids when we heard him announce:

'So I said to myself, what to get the love of your life for her birthday?' Mum wasn't buying into this, and was pulling a nonchalant face with crossed legs and an air of 'What the hell is he going to give me next? I'm already using the Amstrad as a very big paperweight,' but he continued.

'Flowers? Chocolates? No! No! A simple declaration of love is what the doctor ordered! Come out to the courtyard and you'll see!'

We lived in a block with a communal courtyard-cum-car park and although we lived on the ground floor, the block stretched three storeys high. We knew some of our neighbours, but with so many kids screeching around you can bet they all knew who we were. We all went out of the back door to see what Dad had got up to. Dad was ushering Mum at the front of the pack with Jonny, Natalie and Maxine dragging the five of us kids behind them. Stella was still dancing, though, and so she glided out of her own accord.

As we proceeded into the courtyard we could see Mum and Dad's faces first of all. And their mouths were hanging open. I guess Dad had set this all up beforehand because there, standing in the middle of the car park, was a beautiful new-ish car. A rusty off-white Citroen BX GT.

Stella, being a typical girl, couldn't care less, and after a brief glance at the car carried on dancing to the music in her head. But both my older brother Albert and I ran up to it and danced around the new car with Albert shouting out, 'Yo! I got a car! Take that!' Why was Dad showing off? I wondered. Maybe he'd done something really bad, like had an affair or gambled all of our little money away on the horses. Maybe it was Jonny and Natalie who had put him up to making this grand gesture, which was so unlike him.

It was only then that we noticed that Mum and Dad's faces hadn't changed. Dad slowly closed his mouth but instead of a smile I could see a thousand words playing themselves across his lips, jumbled frantically. I followed his gaze and saw something in the bottom right corner of the bonnet that looked ugly and out of place. Someone had defaced the car with smeared black paint. They'd printed a special message for us on the nearly new Amos-mobile. The message read: 'No Blacks. No Irish. No Dogs.'

Ashen, I could see those six words painfully stamped on my dad's consciousness. There was a heartbeat when I thought that anything could happen and for the first time in my life I was afraid of my father. I was afraid of what he might do or say as his proud gesture of love had been hijacked so ignorantly in his own home by a stranger.

Natalie and Jonny looked like they were about to explode with rage as well, but it was Maxine who was first out with a piercing 'BASTARDS! YOU IGNORANT BASTARDS! HOW COULD YOU? HOW COULD YOU? YOU COWARDS!' The worst part was that I had a hunch as to who was responsible. It was the neighbouring family on the other side who had never said a word to us, ever, since we moved in, and whose kids avoided us in the courtyard.

My little brother Chris, who was seven at the time, came up to me and asked innocently, 'Are there wild, black, Irish dogs around the neighbourhood?'

Maxine shook her fist lamely and ran to the racist neighbour in question's communal front door and started hammering at it wildly. 'COME OUT AND SHOW YOURSELVES!' A little old lady battering someone's front door like a madwoman! I'd never seen a white person act like that before. It was frightening to see so much anger and passion stirred up in Maxine's slight frame. So it looked like white people could be terrifying too. Seeing Maxine like that dampened the anger in my dad's face. My mother went up to her, took her by the hand and said, 'Come back into the house. Don't waste your breath on these cowardly people. They simply want to frighten us without showing their faces. As we say in Nigeria,

"When the mouse laughs at the cat, there is a hole nearby.'"

'You know they're SCUM.' Maxine aimed that last word squarely at the front door, which remained closed. 'We're not all like that.'

'Ah! We're not upset. Come inside.' Mum put her arm over Maxine's shoulder and gave it a tight squeeze as she led her back to the flat. Then I saw Mum pass Dad a furtive glance and, as their eyes met, although they said nothing the silence spoke volumes. Were they really going to have to spend their lives moving from one place to another and never find any kind of peace? Nowhere where they could just live happily and fit in?

Once we were inside Dad and Jonny went about cleaning the paint off the car bonnet as surely as if they were cleaning a blocked sewer or bursting a canker sore. A dirty job to be completed quickly and without comment. By the time they came back in the front room, Stella and Natalie had resumed their impromptu 5 Star sing-along. They weren't subdued and if anything they were singing even louder than before. We were all trying to act as if nothing had happened. Mum served us all tea sweetened with condensed milk. But old Maxine was drinking coffee, black and bitter. She sat on a chair in a corner and looked so sad and really ashamed. It was clear that seeing this episode first-hand and in front of a black family who she considered friends had had a profound effect on her. Being of a different generation, perhaps she was remembering the number of times she'd seen signs like that on front doors of hotels and shops and thought nothing of it. Who knows? Ten years before she might have even shared those views or hung a sign like that herself. But Stella danced on.

('So here's the answer to your queeeeeeestion. I want you ALL to myself. Cos I'm . . . ooooh, so go-od. GOOD for you. No! One! Else! Will! Ever! Do-o.)

1

I REMEMBER MY FIRST DAY at school, when I was only five years old. It was a primary school in Hammersmith right next door to where we were living at the time. I ran into the classroom and then ran straight home and said, 'Mum, Mum! Apparently there's a black boy in my class! And I can't find him anywhere.'

She sat me down and said, 'Stephen! It is you!'

Mum didn't send me back to that school, but I couldn't keep moving primaries every time someone said something nasty. If I'd done that I'd have been to more schools than there are in London by the time I was ten. Over the next few years I did, in fact, go to half a dozen different primary schools anyway because Dad was constantly uprooting the family and moving us around West London. He fancied himself as a property developer but I thought we were in the Witness Relocation Programme.

Education is very important to my parents. It's the main reason why they chose to leave a good life in Nigeria and relocate to England (the Biafran war might have had something to do with it too). Coming from West Africa to live in Europe was a pretty gutsy move for a young black couple in the late sixties and it must have been a huge culture shock. Although they grew up in the same town in south-west Nigeria, they didn't actually meet until they were in their twenties and living in Lagos, the capital at the time. The Brits only left Nigeria in 1960 and back then Lagos was a pretty funky place. I've seen photos of them before they emigrated and Dad was wearing hipster flares while Mum sported a paisley print dress and massive stilettos. They both looked incredibly skinny and had afro hair. Huge afro hair. After independence, Nigeria was very unstable and Mum and Dad wanted any kids they'd have to enjoy the best future possible, and so they upped sticks and settled here. They used to say that Caribbeans were invited to England for work but Africans were not. We come here for education, so there was no chance of me missing even a day of school no matter what. I never knew what Mum and Dad meant by this anyway, because all the black folks were working as far as I could tell.

When I was eight, Mum and Dad moved south of the river to Wandsworth and I ended up at a primary in Balham, today a nice suburb of London, but back then it had no such glory. In fact, one of the main thoroughfares was and still is Bedford Hill, a tree-lined street that attracted a hell of a lot of traffic due to the fact that it was a neat short cut, was in close proximity to the Common, and boasted more ladies working at night than a northern sausage factory. I stayed at this rowdy primary school until I sat the 11-plus exam and it was there that I had my first real taste of the wild feral children of south London – they made the kids back in Hammersmith look like pussy cats.

Even though we were still at the age to get free cartons of milk in break times there wasn't an innocent angel among us. We used to go through a lot of teachers even then. Normally on the first day of term they would come into class well dressed and wearing make-up, full of smiles, enthusiasm and encouragement for us pupils. By the third or fourth week you'd see them hiding in their cars at 8.30 in the morning and chain smoking. Their hair would be dishevelled and they'd have stopped washing their clothes and started talking to themselves in the corridors.

But when it became clear that we were a failing state primary a new teacher was drafted in and put in personal charge of our class, which was the worst behaved. Miss Robbins was strict, fierce and she didn't like me at all (because even at the age of nine I wouldn't be quiet and pay attention), but she did one thing that I really appreciated and that surprised everyone. One day she turned up to school carrying a cage containing a hamster and installed him at the back of the classroom. She told us it was up to the students to clean the cage, feed and water the hamster every day. She even let us all vote to give him a name – we voted on Penfold, after the *Danger Mouse* character.

When I told Mum that our class had adopted a cute hamster called Penfold she reacted as if I had told her we'd invited a flea farm to come to school. She acted as if there was a nit time bomb ensconced at the back of the classroom ready to infect us all and I had to beg her not to call the school and embarrass me. Instead of calling the headmistress she resolved to just comb my sister's and my hair more mercilessly than usual, claiming to look for lice.

Coming from a country where animals give you malaria, rabies or just bite your head off if you go wandering into the wrong corner of town, it's not surprising that many Nigerians just aren't into keeping animals as pets. I don't want to speak for all Nigerian people; some people keep dogs for guarding their houses or hunting, but if you like dogs because they can bite strangers on sight and hunt down prey in the African wilds you're still a world away from Paris Hilton's handbag Chihuahua.

The European attitude to animals is totally different from the

African point of view, says my dad, and perhaps it's a little bit weird. White people seem to love big, angry, dangerous animals and really want to seize them out of the bush and stick them in freezing cold, drab zoos or maybe make them dance around in circuses. A smart man knows that the best place for a tiger is somewhere very far away. I'm yet to see a Nigerian version of Siegfried and Roy.

Most Africans like to have harmony with the environment, but it takes a colonialist to want to master every last corner of it. Everyone knows that this mad Englishman Charles Darwin went halfway around the world to find lots of new species on a boat called the *Beagle*. What a pioneer! Not everyone knows that he only went on this great voyage of discovery so that he could eat one of every animal that he found. That's just disgusting. It sounds like someone offered him a drunken bet that he took too seriously. He was a bit like an olden days version of Danny Wallace. Go on Darwin! Eat that ugly tortoise! It took a white person to set up the first protected nature reserves in Africa. But what did people do all day in these early reserves? Well, they shot animals while speeding around on pick-up trucks, drinking beer and acting like they own the place. Barbaric! Although not totally unexpected.

But I love animals a lot and I would dearly have loved to own a pet when I was growing up. However with Mum and Dad around there was no chance of that happening. Whenever we moved house, Mum was constantly fighting a battle to make sure that any kind of rat, mouse, cockroach or anything else that crawled on four legs (apart from my youngest sister) moved out of the house as soon as we moved in. The idea of actually inviting an animal into the house was a bad joke to her. 'If you want to clean up after an animal or feed a mewling, dribbling, hungry mouth, then here! Just look after your sister for an hour.'

By getting a hamster for the class I think the teacher was trying to teach us responsibility. Looking back, I'm amazed that she actually allowed us to look after a living animal, since we spent most of the rest of the time fighting amongst ourselves and pulling chairs out from underneath each other. Let's just say hangman wasn't a word-building game in our school, unless the vocabulary you are building is 'Quick the teacher's coming! Get him down! Get him down! Stop crying, Stephen! You better not tell anyone about this or you're dead meat!'

I remember one girl, Sarah, who was easily the most annoying person in the class, with a whiny voice and bipolar temperament. Even at the tender age of nine, it was clear to see that she'd end up with a few failed marriages and an addiction. She asked one morning:

'Miss, why do we do finger painting? It's dirty and stupid.'

'Why?' enquired Miss Robbins, trying to conceal her frustration at yet another precocious question. 'It's so we can have a record of all your fingerprints . . . early!'

This funny little quip was probably not lost on most of the kids in school. I was definitely in the minority having both of my parents married, still together and neither of them in Wandsworth Prison.

There was one nasty little criminal in the making called Keith whose fingerprints and DNA were destined to be taken many times in his life. Keith was a bully. He was strong. He was dumb. He was ugly. He was horrible to everyone and commanded fear in most of the rest of the kids. He was the best at hiding itching powder in your jacket. He was good at going through your coat pockets where they hung up by the door looking for sweets or money. He used to hang up my coat from the hook by the door . . . Not very nice, because I was still in it at the time.

In spite of the challenging environment the little hamster was well cared for by the pupils. Everyone gave him little scraps of food from their packed lunches and when he started to get too fat we clubbed together and bought a little hamster wheel and put it in his cage.

Apart from his generally furry innocence and friendly character, the very best thing about Penfold was that it turned out bipolar Sarah was allergic to him. If she got a whiff of his rodenty behind she'd start sneezing uncontrollably and her eyes would water and go red. The upshot of this was that she wouldn't come within ten feet of the back of the classroom, where I sat. So not only was he a little ball of fun at the back of the classroom, whirling around on his squeaky wheel, but he was also a four-legged snub-nosed Sarah repellent.

Because I always sat at the back, Penfold and I got to know each other very well during this time. I was fascinated by how he used to eat crumbs and seeds by scooping them in front of his pink twitching nose with his little paws before gobbling them down. He'd always try and burrow under his newspaper bed when we had maths, the most boring class. But when we had art and all the kids were busy with paints, glue, dried pasta and crumpled-up bits of tracing paper he'd come out of hiding and go whizzing round on his squeaky wheel. Even though he was small, he was a very sensitive animal and he could pick up exactly on the mood in the class and join in.

The only kid apart from Sarah who didn't like Penfold was Keith. He was a sadist and was always trying to poke the hamster with a pencil or scoop him out of the cage for some evil purpose. Stella and I were normally on hand to stop him from doing any lasting damage. When it became clear that Sarah was allergic to Penfold, I could see Keith's slug-like brain behind his beady little eyes trying to squeeze out a horrible way to take advantage of this fact. Sarah may have been whiny and a bit wheezy if she got too close to Penfold, but Keith was a much worse character.

One morning I should have realized something was up when halfway through the first lesson Sarah's nose started to drip uncontrollably. By the end of the lesson, she was sneezing every thirty seconds and her eyes were bright red. Miss Robbins decided to take Penfold to the staff room for the rest of the day, much to my distress. I never liked to let him out of my sight when I was in school. But far from improving, Sarah got worse all day until no one could do any work without the ah-ah-ah-tishoo sound punctuated by the slurp of a really disgusting snot-filled sniff. By lunchtime, she was in such a bad state that she had to be sent to the nurse. The teacher went over to Sarah's desk and opened it up only to find handfuls of scrunched-up newspaper taken from Penfold's cage buried under her books at the bottom.

No one admitted to it, but I knew it was Keith who had done it. He mercilessly teased Sarah about her big panda eyes when she came back to class and for the rest of the week he kept doing fake sneezes and sniffles to get under her skin. Bipolar Sarah was not called bipolar Sarah for no reason. She rose to the bait in a big way. She would start crying when Keith provoked her. Or she'd call on the teacher when he threw some balled-up paper at her. Or she'd throw a tantrum when he blew his nose extra theatrically. It got to the point where no one in the class could make even the smallest sound without Sarah thinking someone was making fun of her.

It wasn't funny at all to see a nine-year-old have a mini nervous breakdown whenever someone scraped their chair or coughed. If someone whispered to their neighbour asking to borrow a pencil she'd glare at them with real hatred in her eyes. Sarah was so paranoid that she thought the whole class and even the teacher were against her. When Miss Robbins got some chalk dust up her nose and sneezed, Sarah jumped right up and screamed, 'I hate that hamster,' before pelting out of the room in tears.

By Thursday, the teacher said that she was going to take Penfold home at the weekend and not bring him back because he was causing so much grief in class. I was heartbroken because I swear we had grown to be friends during those long boring lessons in maths, geography and English. I hated Keith at that point; because of him I was going to lose my best distraction and I'd have to go back to counting the ceiling tiles and staring blankly at the clock on the wall.

I resolved to make the most of the rest of the week by playing with Penfold at every opportunity. I even broke the golden rule of class by letting him out of his cage at break time on Friday and cradling him in my arms along with a few of the other kids. Passing him from hand to hand; giving his tummy a rub; feeling his tiny heart thumping a mile a minute; feeding him bits of sandwich. That little critter had never had so much attention its life. In the corner of the classroom, however, far away from the rest of us playing around with Penfold, sat Keith staring at us and biting his nails. He used to bite them right down to the skin. It was disgusting.

After lunch on Friday we had double art, which was always a nice way to see us off into the weekend. We were all given a set of paints and a blank piece of paper and told to do self-portraits. This was more Miss Robbins's doing. Before she had turned up, art classes consisted of the serious job of cutting a potato in half and making prints on coloured card (teachers in those days really didn't have to be much more clued up than the kids they were teaching). I was making a mess of things and producing something that

Picasso would not have been proud of when I noticed that there was something missing. Where was the usual squeak, squeak, squeak of the hamster wheel? Where was Penfold? I turned and went over to the cage but he was nowhere to be seen. He wasn't on his wheel. He wasn't hiding under the newspaper. He was gone!

'Miss! Miss! Penfold's gone! Where's Penfold?'

Miss Robbins came to the back of the room and looked worriedly at the empty cage. 'He must have got out. Can anyone see him?'

Of course all the kids started running around the classroom like headless chickens calling out, 'Penfold! Penfold!' and generally revelling in the distraction. All except for Sarah who definitely didn't care about the hamster and who, after a week of suffering persecutions (some imaginary, some real – she really was very annoying), was beginning to look a lot like Private Pile out of *Full Metal Jacket* just before he loses it and goes on a killing spree.

'Get back to your desks this minute,' commanded Miss Robbins, trying to regain control of a bunch of overexcited and delinquent children.

'Maybe Stephen's got him inside his desk. We all know that Stephen's gay for Penfold,' spat Keith.

'Am not, miss! Take that back.' I was only nine years old.

'Be quiet, Keith. Everyone check inside your desks.' An unholy racket of desks slamming open and shut ensued for a few minutes as all the kids took advantage of the chance to further disrupt the class.

When the teacher finally regained control, Keith said slyly, 'Miss Robbins, Sarah's not checked her desk yet.'

'Sarah! Just look inside!' cried an exasperated Miss Robbins. Sarah opened her hinged wooden desktop and uttered a piercing scream as poor Penfold's nose gently emerged from the lip of her desk. He must have been terrified in the dark wooden desk with all the noise in the room and, as he tried to escape, Sarah threw the desk lid down on top of him and we all heard a horrible crunch. A red wet matted patch of fur was crushed under the lid and everyone fell silent in shock. Everyone except for Keith who cackled with laughter, slamming his desk top up and down and pointing at Sarah, who was completely horrified.

What happened next confirmed my suspicion that Sarah was a bit unhinged herself. She let out a hateful scream and sprinted across the room to Keith where she began to beat him with closed fists. It took the teacher to pull Sarah off of Keith as she pulled his hair, yanking his head from side to side. And I mean the teacher literally pulled Sarah into the air with a fistful of Keith's black hair in her fist.

Once free, Keith was clearly dazed and bruised around the temples. He staggered around a bit and cradled his neck, trying to make sure his head was in fact still attached to his body. He saw the whole class looking at him with total hate. Well, I don't know about anyone else, but I was definitely giving him the evil eye. He did what all cowardly bullies do. He lied straight through his teeth. 'It wasn't me! Stop looking at me like that! I didn't do anything! I don't know how that rat got in her desk!' Maybe the beating he'd sustained had knocked his senses out of whack – if he ever had any to start with. He could see that the whole class was against him.

Forget potato printing. That day I learned a lesson in how the line blurs between doing mischief and doing something really really bad. It was a line that he would go on to cross plenty of times in later life I was sure. I could see his face harden then and there and he went from being a naughty kid to being a criminal-minded bastard. He'd killed a defenceless little creature and whatever light of innocence he had went out in his eyes. I could see straight through his head as he stared down the class of horrified nine-year-olds. His little reptile brain was working away but there was nothing good left in there. I mean the wheel was turning, but the hamster was truly dead.

Keith may have been trying to play a joke but had ended up murdering Penfold and sending Sarah right over the edge. When you are grown up and run into people you went to school with everyone probes around a bit to try and find out how everyone changed. Nowadays, with things like Facebook, it's even easier, and even I've been known to lurk around to see what people got up to. Ugly kids got married and had children. Bullied kids got jobs and went on to be happy. Quiet kids moved abroad. Nobody knows what Keith is up to now because he doesn't have a Facebook page. Well, you're not allowed to have one in prison.

2

BACK IN THE EARLY EIGHTIES there were only a handful of black kids around, and two of them were me and my twin sister. It would be a few years until the younger siblings would be able to join us, and my brother Albert, who was three years older, was already at a secondary grammar school. So we had to come up with survival strategies to get by in those first few shaky years. The best tactic was to meet up in break and talk about who had been really horrible, then my sister would crouch behind them and I'd push them over her. It was hilarious and it always worked. It was at primary school that I first started to become the typical class clown. Well, you have to see the funny side when kids were coming up to you and saying things like 'Do black people wash their hair?' My answer: 'Why no! We stand outside and wait for it to rain.'

And the teachers weren't much better. When I did my 11-plus exam, I got good enough grades to make it to a grammar school. But when I had a conversation with my careers advisor, he said, 'Hmmm, you could be a bus conductor, a chef? How about a runner? You people run, don't you? Run! Run!' These were the kind of teachers who if Barack Obama had said that he wanted to be the world's top politician, he'd have been told, 'Hmm, well

I can definitely see you on a campaign bus, but only if you're driving it.'

I was very pleased to take my 11-plus and leave that particular primary school behind. It was expected that most of the kids would go on to the local secondary modern school or, more likely, borstal. The only reason I passed the exam was because of my sister. She had studied hard and never taken any notice of the other kids at school. All the teachers thought that she'd get into the local grammar school easily, but she desperately wanted me to get in too so that she wouldn't be alone in class.

So she tried to tutor me. Now, if I don't pay attention in class with an adult at the front harassing me to learn my nine times table then I definitely wasn't going to perform any better for Stella. After a while she realized that it was going to be impossible for me to get up to date with the curriculum. I literally knew nothing. She asked me to my face how it was that I hadn't picked up on anything in class. Then she asked me who was tying my shoelaces every morning because apart from in reading and writing I displayed the knowledge of a five-year-old.

'Stephen, what is hard water?'

'Ice.'

'What do you need for photosynthesis?'

'A darkroom.'

'Where do you find chlorophyll?'

'Swimming pools.'

'Stephen, describe this graph.'

'It's very pretty.'

'What's pi for?'

'Dinner.'

'Stephen, do you know the name of our teacher?'

'Yes. Miss Robbins.'

'So you have been in the class, but Stephen, how have you managed not to fail every single test we've ever been set?'

So I told her my secret. The way I'd been getting the answers in school tests was this: I had been cheating. I used to look at the back of the other kids' pencils and work out what they were writing from the squiggles and loops they made in the air. I thought she was going to lay into me for being a cheater but she actually looked impressed.

'Stephen, you should work for the secret service or something because that is wicked. Do you ever look at my pencil?' I felt guilty telling Stella that she was my number one copy buddy and she didn't even know it. Stella was never in trouble with any teachers, but because we were twins the teachers separated us for tests. They used to say that we were 'thick as thieves' even though we were not up to any mischief (at least Stella wasn't). In fact it was easier to clock the back of someone's pencil if they were a few rows away than if they were right next to you. So using this technique I managed to pass the 11-plus with flying colours and we expected to go to the same school the next year. Which we did, but not in the way we expected to.

About two weeks into the summer holidays Dad announced that we were going to take our first ever family holiday. We assumed that this meant we were going to Peterborough to see some distant cousin of Dad's, but actually it turned out that we were going to get on an aeroplane and fly off to another country. And that country was going to be Nigeria.

Now this news was met with quite a lukewarm reception on our part. It's odd trying to find your identity when you have dual heritage and we never knew exactly what to make of the West African country they had hailed from. All our lives we'd been told we were Nigerian first and British second. But when we asked why we had to live in England, where we were often the subjects of racial abuse, Mum and Dad told us that it was worth it to live in the UK. So we had figured that Nigeria must be really *really* bad if this was the best option.

All we really knew about Nigeria was that it was hot, that everyone there was black, that it used to be British and that there had been a war there. Mum and Dad had purposefully not taught us the Yoruba language, which they spoke privately to each other when they thought we were out of earshot. Both Stella and I had actually picked some of it up and we realized that when they were speaking it there were normally money worries or children worries under discussion. Those subjects were normally linked together.

'Do not talk like me or your mother or you will never get anywhere in this country,' Dad used to say to us. And so we had grown up on a strict diet of Trevor McDonald, which meant we picked up his accent and also some of his phrases and mannerisms. I would come home from school and say, 'Reports are in. Stephen was late with his homework. Sources suggest he will be in detention next week. My sister has more.'

So the idea of going to this foreign country was both exciting and frightening. I thought that perhaps finally I would fit in. My sister was worried about eating foreign food. Albert hoped that he might meet a nice girl, and the younger kids, Cordelia and Chris, were only four and five years old and so they didn't really understand what was going on.

It was enough of a hassle to actually get there. At the time Nigeria may have been on the British Airways radar but we couldn't afford the UK's national carrier. It came down to a choice between West African Airways or, bizarrely, Aeroflot, the national carrier of Russia. Aeroflot is well known as the death trap of the skies but it actually had a better safety record than West African Airways. However, since Aeroflot meant you had to transfer through Moscow it was decided by Dad that we should go with West African Airways.

We went in two groups. Mum went first with me, Stella and Albert, and Dad was to follow a couple of weeks later with the youngest kids. We were all excited by the idea of getting onto an aeroplane but the actual experience itself seemed a bit strange to me. When we were on board, the safety announcement said that you would find your life jacket under your seat. Your lifejacket under your seat?! All I could think of was, life jacket? Who needs a life jacket on an aeroplane? If this thing's going down I want a parachute. Have they messed up and given all of our parachutes to P&O Cruises? Heads are going to roll if there's an incident, and we don't plunge headlong into the sea.

Thoughts like these were floating around my head when we were strapped in and taking off. And the flight was pretty scary. This was in the days before people hopped on planes for stag nights and a lot of the passengers on the flight were probably flying for the first time. But for me it was very cool. I've always loved cars, trains and, of course, planes. Anything that has a big engine goes fast and makes a noise like 'vroom', I am a fan of.

This plane was not a jumbo jet. It was a small plane. 'A flying coffin', as my mother put it. There was not a lot of room on board and there was a chemical toilet at the back. The on-board meal for us kids consisted of a biscuit and a cup of milk. I've been lucky enough to travel quite a lot as a comedian and I know that proper jet planes ought to go very high. This one flew pretty close to the ground and we could actually see the view of roads and fields as they passed beneath us. The whole country below looked like a patchwork quilt as we flew south towards Africa.

There was a lot of turbulence and before long Stella, Mum and Albert were all being sick into bags. I thought this was pretty funny because Mum had insisted that we all dressed up in our best clothes only for us to be sick all over them. This flight sickness was probably the reason why the airline chose not to give the passengers much to eat once they were on board. Although I reckon Mum's sickness had more to do with her being terrified than the bumpy ride as she kept shouting to no one in particular, 'Fly above the clouds! Fool!' You have to remember that this is a woman whose idea of adventure up until then had been to open the curtains back home and say, 'Look!' before closing them again.

There was no in-flight entertainment except when one Nigerian family began arguing with the stewardess. Now these stewardesses were not the Virgin Atlantic supermodel types. No. They looked like they had rolled out of bed, opened a make-up bag and just dunked their heads into it up to their necks. Customer service is not an idea that has fully percolated down to Africa, and the stewardess gave as good as she got. As I've said, Nigerian people are quick to raise their voices when they are just having a nice chat but when a real argument is in full swing things can get out of hand fast. The captain himself came back at one point and calmed everyone down. '*Abeg, make I hear word!*' which is Pidgin English and roughly translates as 'Please stop arguing or I'll crash the plane.'

When we touched down in Lagos, Nigeria, everyone clapped and few people shouted 'Praise God and *oluwasegun*' ('God has been victorious' in Yoruba). I thought it was pretty strange that they applauded the pilot when he got us safely to our destination. What would they have done if we had crashed? Probably shouted, 'Boo! Hiss!' while reaching for their life jackets.

If you've never been to Nigeria then the first thing you notice is the heat. It's not like English heat at all. It's like sitting in a sauna.

In tropical countries, you feel the heat in your lungs when you breathe in. It's like inhaling something solid and hot. Like a cup of tea going down the wrong way. You even feel like you're going to choke a little bit at first. And this hot, humid, muggy air captures the surrounding smells more strongly than a dry heat. Suddenly, you are aware of the distant smells of cooking and cooking fires and even the smells of the people you're standing next to. It takes some getting used to at first.

The immigration queue was massive and totally out of control, with most of the passengers shouting at each other and at the security guards. These poor guards could hardly control anyone since back then procedure took a back seat to favours, and it wasn't what you knew but who you knew. Everyone in that queue claimed to know someone in authority to ease them into the country, but Mum had a real connection. Her voice rose above the surrounding clamour and one of these guys wearing neat and tidy white uniforms escorted us to the top of the queue. When we got to the border control she took out two passports for each of us. A green Nigerian one and a black British one. She handed the Nigerian passports to the officer and he waved us through, looking wearily at the angry people we'd pushed in front of.

Later Mum told me, 'Remember your roots, Stephen. You are Nigerian first and British second. Except when you are going into Heathrow Airport. Then use the black passport.'

The second thing you notice about Lagos is the amount of people. Even at the airport there were thousands of people getting up to some business or other. There were people cooking barbecued meat and corn. There were people selling beer, water and cola. You could come directly off the plane and immediately buy sandals and African wraps that were more appropriate for the African climate. But by far and away the majority of the people were there to greet arriving relatives by the dozen. As soon as we had our bags in our hands and were out of the terminal, Mum's sister Yomi rushed forward and embraced us each in turn saying, 'God be praised! You have arrived back home at last!'

She bundled us towards the car park where four different cars all packed with different uncles, aunties and cousins were waiting for us. By the time we'd greeted them all another hour had passed. Those who didn't grab us and hug us were the older members of the family and when we offered our hands to them Mum pushed us in the back and said, 'Why don't you prostrate?' And so there, on the car park's dirty muddy ground we had to get down on our hands and knees and prostrate towards these people who I'd never even heard of before. I wasn't sure if I was going to like doing this to everyone I met. But I at least had a good opportunity to muck up my posh clothes.

As we drove away, Albert and I were excited but I could see Stella looking longingly back towards the airport. She was obviously not sure if this was going to be the best holiday after all and she'd have been happier in the UK dreaming of going to big school in the autumn. Things seemed ominous to Stella. She said to me, 'Why did they say welcome home? This place isn't my home at all.'

By the time we were all safely packed into the cars and on the move it was evening and the roads were crowded with people milling around and all different kinds of cars were blaring their horns at each other. It was pitch black and there weren't any streetlights working. The road could only be discerned because of the virtually gridlocked traffic that jammed it up. Without any clear idea of where the kerb and the road met it was pretty obvious that a lot of the cars were just trying to go around the outside and create their own personal hard shoulders. The fires that people had lit by the sides of the road to cook by were the only signs anyone had of where it was safe to go. It was a world away from the A24.

We travelled to a suburb of Lagos called Ikeja where we were to stay with Auntie Yomi. She was Mum's little sister and we'd seen her in a mouldy old photograph that Mum had shown us back in England. She looked just like a young version of Mum and she was full of energy. Most of the other newfound relatives that we'd just met hadn't seemed too friendly and had barely uttered a word when we greeted them, but Yomi went out of her way to talk to us and make us feel comfortable. Even Nigerians know that Lagos can make your head spin and Yomi appreciated how shocking it might seem to kids who'd grown up thousands of miles away.

As we came into the populated areas we saw how people lived. It was sort of like how you'd live in London if it were 45ºC and 100 per cent humidity every day of the year. There were lots of medium-rise city blocks of about six or seven storeys. There might have been enclosed living spaces at the back but all you could see were massive balconies, which were really more like multistorey terraced verandas. People were cooking and washing and talking and drying their clothes in the almost open air. You could see families hanging over the balconies on their verandas calling up and down to each other.

Stella, Albert and I looked out of the window at this vibrant night-time atmosphere, thick with noise and smells, with a kind of excited terror. It was Albert though who first noticed the music. Almost everyone was playing something and the tinny twang of radios and boom boxes competed with people playing guitars and horns. We learned later that Ikeja was the heart of an Afrobeat revolution that was sweeping Nigeria and that had started with the famous Fela Kuti. Immediately, we felt soothed by the rhythm and even Mum, stressed from lugging herself and her kids across a continent, began to relax. By the time we arrived at our auntie's home, everyone in the car was talking and hoping that maybe we'd get a taste of the barbecued meat, called *suya*, that we could smell everywhere.

Lagos is in the same time zone as London and so although Mum must have been knackered by dinner time, we weren't at all. In tropical countries you avoid the heat of the middle of the day and people stay up all night. So the streets were just coming to life as we arrived at Auntie Yomi's detached bungalow. She lived on a private road with a gate and a security guard and once we were inside we noticed that the kitchen and living room were on a covered veranda and only the bedrooms were inside. (We also noticed there were only two bedrooms.) The first thing we did was unpack the cars and get settled – Mum, with Auntie Yomi; Albert, Stella and me all in the other room.

It was pretty obvious that we were too hungry and excited to go to bed and negotiate the delicate sleeping arrangements. Yomi asked us what we all wanted to do for dinner. She offered to start the cooker and make something at home or she said that we could all go out for the night, pick up some food at a local bar and take a look around. Albert and I jumped at the chance to go out and we followed behind Mum and Yomi, with Stella walking between us. We said that we'd keep close to Stella who was still nervous of the assault against the senses, but actually in this alien environment we were all happy to stick together. It was, after all, a very strange place for three kids who had been discouraged from going out after dark even in London.

We got to the local bar and nobody seemed to care that three underage kids had just walked in. When the barwoman saw Auntie Yomi she shouted, 'Ay, sista! *Wetin dey happen?*'

In Nigeria there are lots of different languages but Yoruba is the main language in the south-west where Lagos is. But to make things a bit easier everyone across the whole of Nigeria speaks this Pidgin English. '*Wetin dey happen*?' was a common greeting in Pidgin English that we'd have to get used to.

'How now, sista? *Nottin dey happen.*'

We edged into the packed bar and a couple of rowdy customers even grabbed Albert, who was fourteen, and offered him a Gulder beer. Auntie Yomi was having none of it and swooped in to grab Albert away and berate the man in Yoruba: '*Ay Ay! Kilo ndamu e? Odomode okunrin mi niyi!*' 'What's wrong with you? This is my boy!' Mum translated.

'Ay, sista! *Ema binu.*' He apologized and looked at me. 'Broda. I am sorry. *Abeg no put me for trouble.*'

I looked up at Mum who stared back at me looking angry. I thought I'd probably done something wrong and was about to prostrate myself, but before I could Mum pulled me up by the scruff of my shirt and ushered us all to a table near the bar. It was a strange thing to see because Mum had always told us never to be rude to older people and to treat them with a lot of respect. It looked like maybe things had changed in Nigeria since Mum and Dad had left.

'Ay Yomi, sista, what has happened to Ikeja? All this hustle and bustle. These bars and music everywhere.'

'Oh yes!' cried Yomi. 'The people here. They are always drinking, drinking. *Ori e o pe!* Their head is not correct! But don't worry we will eat our fill here. The cook is one of the best in Ikeja. It may be a little bit spicy but I hope your children are not all too soft for it.' She poked Albert in the stomach. 'Or are you a butter eater, boy?' and laughed.

Nigerian food takes some getting used to. It normally means a spicy stew of meat and vegetables and you eat with it something that, at first glance, looks a bit like paste. Paste is a word that you should encounter after 'tooth' or 'wallpaper', not before dessert. I asked my Auntie Yomi, 'What is this paste?' and she looked dumbfounded. 'This is not paste, it is *eba*, like *egusi*, *amala* or *garri*.' It seemed to me like that was a lot of words for the same thing. *Garri* is a bit like semolina, and it is an acquired taste, to say the least. And you don't use a spoon, a knife, or a fork to eat it with. You use your hands. You have to pick up some of the paste between your thumb and forefingers, make a well in the middle of it and scoop the stew up into it, and then into your mouth in one smooth movement.

Eating with *garri* is a food fight waiting to happen. And in mine and Albert's case it very soon degenerated into just that. Stella looked on in horror as we slowly caked our hands in *garri* up to the wrist with more *garri* around our mouths, chins and shirts. Mum and Yomi sipped Gulder beers and we drank cola from glass bottles to quench the fire of the spicy stew in our bellies. Poor Stella couldn't handle the spices and perked up only when they bought out skewers of barbecued *suya*, which she gratefully tucked into with abandon.

With our bellies full, we all left the bar and started to wander back towards Yomi's house just as the streets were getting even more busy with customers looking for food, drink and a party. The Afrobeat music we'd heard as we'd arrived was now everywhere and some sound systems had been set up in different quarters of the neighbourhood with amplifiers rigged up to the exposed overhead wiring to get power. Big fires and strings of bright multicoloured lights popped up near the sound systems and crowds were gathering to dance to the music.

It was still about 30ºC degrees out as we stepped onto the

veranda at Auntie Yomi's place. She put on a pot of water and made us all hot tea before going to bed.

Mum took her tea from Yomi and gestured towards the street and the thumping sound systems. 'Sista, how long will this racket be playing for?'

'There are big parties around here and they will go on all night. You can hear them every night. Even Sunday.'

'Even on Sunday? Don't people know when enough is enough?'

'Ah! You can go to church and head straight back out to dance and drink some more,' said Yomi with a smile.

'They should pray to God for forgiveness. Drinking all night? The death that will kill a man begins as an appetite. It's too much. And what about the children? Will they be safe?'

'Of course. We have security twenty-four-seven on this road.' Yomi turned to us. 'Just don't head outside and go wandering around until the sun is out unless you are with me or your mummy.'

'Ah! If I so much as see you off this veranda without me I will beat you!' It was a bit strange seeing Mum acting like this. I don't mean it was strange for her to say that she'd beat us; she did that all the time in London. But I'd never heard her talking about Sunday as being anything special and back home we almost never went to church.

The tea settled our stomachs after all the spicy food and we slowly began to yawn and look to the bedroom. Mum tucked us into bed. It wasn't like being tucked up at home under sheets and blankets. In Ikeja you get tucked away under mosquito nets and it's best to sleep on top of the sheets. We lay there with the smell of Nigeria in our noses and the beat of Afrobeat music echoing away in the distance lulling us to sleep.

3

YOMI TURNED OUT TO be the archetypal funky aunt. She kept us entertained at her place in Ikeja for two weeks, during which time we were always out visiting people or having people around. She loved music and was really well connected to the Afrobeat scene. My mum's family is related to Fela Kuti and Yomi had known him very well when he lived in Nigeria before he became an international superstar. Fela came from the same small town about an hour and a half north of Lagos that my family originated from. The town is called Abeokuta, which means 'under the rock'. It's not as bad as it sounds; everyone's not running about under a rock like a bunch of woodlice or ants. The name comes from a massive mountain that sits above the town and lots of famous Nigerians come from Abeokuta including Fela, Wole Soyinka, the first African Nobel-prize winner for literature, and Olusegun Obasanjo, the famous Nigeria president. (And me.)

Although it's not rich, Nigeria consistently rates as one of the happiest nations on Earth. We have the biggest economy in Africa and we have the first African Nobel laureate. The average Nigerian can speak three languages whereas most of my friends back home in London could barely master one – 'Yeah, man I want a burger and put sauce init. No not init. Just put sauce init. Not in the burger just on the side init. No not init, init?' There are in fact many valuable things that the rest of the world could take from Nigeria. And I don't just mean the vast oil reserves in the south.

Lagos isn't what you'd call a tourist town in the traditional sense, but there is a lot to see if you keep your eyes open. And you'd better keep your eyes open or you'll get hit by a truck. It's a busy place, and just looking at the life going on around you can be interesting and a little bit scary. For example, until I'd visited the local market I'd never seen a goat walking down the street or a chicken killed and gutted before my very eyes to be cooked that night. In spite of sitting on top of tons of oil, Nigeria doesn't have a steady power supply and a blackout can last anywhere from two hours to two days, so refrigerate anything fresh at your peril. To make sure the meat doesn't go bad before you eat it people just keep the animal alive until the last possible moment.

When we were in Nigeria the power company was called NEPA and it was dreadfully unreliable. It was a regular thing to hear people complain that 'NEPA has taken the light'. Even today it's not much better. The new power company is called the Power Holding Company of Nigeria or PHCN, but everyone translates it as Please Hold Candle in Nigeria. To make up for this, like a lot of people, Yomi had a big petrol generator at her house and so we could have lights and even watch TV whenever we wanted.

Nigerian television is dominated by Nollywood, which is now the world's second biggest film industry. Nigeria has a strong story-telling tradition and so it's natural that we should have a big film industry. However we also have a big culture of '*tatafo*', which means gossip. The problem is when these two worlds collide. 'Ah!

You are going to see *ET*? Come here I want to tell you something
. . . He goes home! . . .' 'You want to see *Gone With the Wind*?
Pssst . . . He doesn't give a damn!'. . . '*Star Wars*? . . . Darth Vader?
He's Luke's father!'

Another thing you notice in a city of industry and action is
everyone going to and from their working enterprises, and that
means a lot people travelling around on foot and on the roads.
Now, you have to be a bit of a thrill seeker to drive in Lagos. You
can just buy a driving licence from the right people, traffic lights
are few and far between, and I don't think I ever saw a zebra
crossing. However, in a weird quaint little throwback from the
colonial days there are traffic policemen in white cotton gloves who
try to direct the madness without getting sideswiped.

Because the traffic is so bad, the main way that people get
around is on motorbikes called *okadas*. Everyone who drives them
weaves them in and out of traffic and they are just as crazy as the
car drivers – although they're a lot faster. In England you may see
two people riding on a motorbike seat; in Nigeria you will regularly
see Daddy, Mummy, two kids and a goat on a single wobbly
motorbike. And just as people load vans with goods in the UK,
people balance boxes of food, TVs or whatever else on the *okadas*.
The best sight I ever saw was someone travelling on one of these
motorbikes with a full-sized coffin strapped to it. I don't know if
he was an undertaker by trade or if it was just the Nigerian version
of motor insurance.

In Ikeja we were all getting into the swing of things. When
people said they'd come around for dinner at seven o'clock, they
really meant they'd arrive at eleven. When people said that a
chicken cost 150 naira, they meant that it really cost 50 naira. We
learned that if you're driving along and a policeman stops you and
says, 'Hello, dear, I hope you have a nice day.' What he really

means is 'Hello, dear, I hope you have a nice day and give me 50 naira, or you won't.'

With so many people coming into the house day and night, we learned a lot of Pidgin English and a lot of Yoruba cuss words. The most frequent of which was the *Ori e o pe* phrase, which means 'his head is not correct'. Yoruba is full of weird and wonderful phrases like that and I asked Yomi why she used that particular saying so much. She acted shocked and looked at me like I was a true fool.

'You butter-eater English-educated boy. You mean that you don't even know the story of where you came from? Don't you know that when the god Olodumare decides to do his job of making the Yoruba people, their headless bodies are made first and then each person chooses his own head. So when you pick a good head at birth then your destiny will be to have luck, fame and good fortune. But if you don't even have the sense to pick the right kind of head then you are a real *were*-fool. We say that the stupidest man is *Oloriburuku*, a person with a bad head. For everyone else you can just say *Ori e o pe*, his head is not correct.'

After two weeks in Ikeja we were getting used being a bit of a novelty in the area and the arrival of Dad with Chris and Cordelia was a bit of a shock. He brought with him the stark reminder of home, not just because he was the newest arrival but because he'd brought a massive amount of luggage with him. Of course, as I have already said, he is a serial hoarder, but he pulled up to Yomi's bungalow in a van filled to the brim with bags, boxes and cases. When he finally came into the bungalow, he greeted his sister-in-law and immediately began complaining about the cost of coming over from England.

'Sista Yomi, *how you dey?*' he said in Pidgin to her.

'Since the children arrived in my home we have visitors every day. *Everybody don dey hala.*' Everybody's been coming around and having a party, she replied with a smile. 'You lookin vex, Mr Man. *Somtin dey worry you?*'

'Ah! To get all these bags through customs I had to pay and pay and pay. Every big eye man chop my money.'

'Yes. Where will you unpack so much? There's not enough room here for all of that.'

'No, sista. We're going to go stay another place. Come on, everybody. Get packed up quick and get ready. Come on. Come on! *Put leg for road!*' This was an unexpected annoyance. We'd been having a nice time with Yomi and her friends. Stella was even getting used to the food here and suddenly Dad arrives from home with screaming kids, too much stuff as usual, and now we had to pack up and go stay with him somewhere else? This was too much. We were pretty sad to lug our bags outside and squish up together in the back of the overheated, non-air-conditioned rusty old van and say goodbye to Yomi.

'It go better now your daddy's here! I'll see you.' Yomi waved as we drove off into the Lagos streets.

Dad was full of curses as he tried to manage driving around the city for the first time in twenty years. He seemed to know where he was going, which was good, but he kept complaining that the roads were so much busier than they used to be.

'These ugly *were* drivers! Are they trying to kill us? With so many cars on the road there is nobody even (HONK!) paying attention to where they are going.'

We wound around the city on the big multi-lane highways freely changing from one lane to another. Dad watched in horror as other drivers simply drove on the wrong side of the road to avoid a traffic queue or a pothole. We had just gotten used to it over the last fortnight and so laughed at Dad who seemed to be so maddened by the whole thing. He didn't laugh at all and glared at us so we shut up pretty quickly.

He finally stopped the car about halfway down a dusty side road that branched off a huge highway. This was no private gate and there was no smartly dressed security guard to greet us as we got out of the rusty old van, which he had parked in front of a two-storey stone house that looked like it had seen better days. This was an odd move on Dad's part and it wasn't lost on Albert, Stella and me. On the way here, we'd wondered if he was driving us to a hotel or to another relative or to a storage place. Instead he'd brought us to an unfurnished house with a well in the back and no TV.

It was in a suburb called Orile Iganmu and it felt very far from Ikeja. It looked like there weren't going to be a lot of sound system parties in this drab part of town. It did not seem like a good place to take a holiday at all, but we didn't have time to dwell on it too much as box after box was thrust into our hands and we set about unpacking. It took all day to get all the boxes unpacked with Mum rushing around, sweeping the floors, opening the windows and trying to air out the house. By the end of the day, the place was beginning to look a bit more like home. Not home in the 'There's no place like home' Dorothy kind of way. I mean it began to look like our home in London as in cluttered and chaotic. Mum fetched water from the well and fed us all bowls of *garri* and spiced stew for dinner and we ate it quickly and quietly before bedding down for the night.

The next day, Albert, Stella and I had to get out of bed early and dress up in nice clothes. It was a Monday morning and so we knew we weren't going to visit friends or head to church. The penny really dropped when Dad took us out in the now empty but still rusty van and stopped outside a school. As Dad ushered the three of us out of the van and into the school reception, a crowd of uniformed school kids appeared and curiously stared at us. Stella was the first to figure out what was going on and burst into tears. Dad started to sign a lot of papers and we realized that we were not going to be heading back to England any time soon. All the hard work that she'd put into getting good grades in her 11-plus, and even in getting me to pass the exam, seemed to have been totally in vain. Even the secondary comprehensive was preferable to this. However, it looked like she would at least get her wish of having us go to the same school when term started.

4

MANY THOUGHTS WERE GOING around inside my head. Nigeria. Naija. Niajaland. Yoruba. Hausa. Igbo. Jai! Shut up you dirty stinking mout' that you've never washed since the day you were born in the gutter! Don't tell me that I have to live here!

Stella, Albert and I sat together that night and we couldn't believe that Mum and Dad had taken us to live here without even telling us. Why did we get no warning? If I had known I may have tried to run away again. I had already tried it once in London. Well, I walked. The phrase 'run away' implies that there was someone running behind me shouting, 'Come back, come back! I love you!' which there wasn't. I went back home after it got dark and nobody had even noticed that I had left. You don't know what its like growing up with seven people sitting around the dinner table and your mum asks your brother while pointing to you, 'Hey, who's your friend?' In a big family your parents can neglect you all and call it economy of scale.

So we'd gone from Londoners to Lagosians overnight. We didn't have any time to get adjusted to anything because a week after Dad enrolled us in school we had to start. The Nigerian school year runs from January to December, so we were going straight into the second term. Stella and I would be in the same secondary entry-level class and Albert was going into the more senior class three years ahead of us. So to add insult to injury, we were going to miss out on our summer holidays altogether. We were given bolts of cloth in the school colours and we had to pay someone to make our uniforms. It was like a condemned man being made to pay for his own bullet. That first day was a horrible experience, and the heat on the mile-long walk to school produced more sweat than I'd ever known.

A kid going into the school class halfway through the year is already social suicide. But we weren't just new; we were foreign to the other kids and to the teachers too. My Nigerian roots are important to me, but simply having black skin does not qualify you for fitting perfectly in to a foreign culture with its fair share of bullies. They taught in English but they mainly spoke Pidgin English and Yoruba in break and at lunch and we could barely understand them. With our English accents we did not fit in any better here than we had back home in South London.

By the time we had been in Orile Iganmu for a month our home was quite comfortable. We had electricity when NEPA hadn't taken the light, and we had clean water from the well, a TV and radio, a cooker and beds. But the school was a complete eye-opener, with no windows and just a door-sized hole where a door should have been as an entrance. There was no power and so no air conditioning or fans and because the tropical heat of the day ran from six thirty in the morning until two in the afternoon. We had to leave every day at first light, which is the only option as there is barely any street lighting in Lagos but there are a lot of very deep potholes. And the food from the school kitchen was so bad that we had to go out and buy *suya* from the local *suya* spot for lunch every day.

We thought that with our English education we would at least be at the top of the class, but we were wrong. They were not only at a higher level than us in science and maths but they also had classes in subjects that we had never encountered before – like agriculture. By which I mean we had to actually plough the land and plant seeds. With the teachers barking at us for getting it wrong and sweating in our uncomfortable uniforms, Stella and I felt like we were on a chain gang. And the religious education was not like I'd experienced it in the UK. It wasn't a philosophical debate class or even a history of the Bible. It was just a prayer group led by a local preacher. First, we had to read the Bible for half an hour, then we had to pray to the Lord while shaking our heads from side to side like possessed people. This is supposed to shake out the bad thoughts! To me this seemed odd. At school I didn't cry for three days because I thought I was having a nightmare.

Back home in London, the other kids and the teachers had been the major problem for me, but here it was the schoolmasters. Nigeria has rejected so much of British culture but has kept some strange archaic bits and pieces almost at random. The schoolmaster is one of these. They aren't teachers, more like school housemasters and administrators, and they look after the boarding houses. A lot of Nigerian schools have boarding houses attached to them because so many families live in rural areas and need to send their children to cities and towns for education.

In most ways, boarding-school pupils in Nigeria are not like the English equivalent at all. The kids are not aristocratic, rich and pampered. It is completely the opposite. The kids in the boarding houses are the poorer kids and they make fun of the day students as being a bunch of soft, indulged *ajebo or ajebutta* (butter eaters). However, in other ways, the boarding house regime is a lot like

45

that found in English boarding schools. As in the experience is a living hell for the kids who live there.

Everyone is terrified of the housemasters because they are liberal users of corporal punishment and they use sticks, cowhide and *kobokos* (whips) to flog the students. Even the other teachers were completely terrified of them. So much so that I guessed that some of the junior teachers were being regularly flogged by these grotesque creatures. Going to school in Nigeria is really like something out of a Roald Dahl book.

Soon after we moved to Orile Iganmu, my dad's mother, Mama Bunmi, came to stay with us. Her family were from all over West Africa, which meant that she could speak a dozen languages and was such easy company that everyone in the area seemed to know her. I remember the day she arrived very well because Dad stood outside waiting for her for over an hour and cried when she arrived. She came on foot, which was strange because we basically lived off a highway, but she must have come via a market because her bag was brimming with fruit for all of us kids. Mum's family are all tall and rangy and there are a lot of them (all of the relatives who'd come to meet us at the airport were from her side), but Dad's side are shorter, broader and quick to smile. When we started to prostrate before her, she grabbed us up before we hit the ground and hugged us all at once.

She had come to our home to help look after the youngest kids, but she would often come and pick us up from school and accompany us home. When Mama Bunmi saw the kind of food that the school kitchen served she was appalled and made friends with the local *suya* seller, who agreed to give us food and water whenever we were hungry. Granny agreed to settle the bill at the end of each month because she was a much better haggler than we were. Everything in Nigeria is about haggling and she told us the secret. 'In this city you can pay in money or in talk-time. I am an old woman and have a lot of time on my hands. The longer you talk the lower the price!'

Things were not going that well at home. Mum and Dad were not rich by Nigerian standards at all. We didn't have a private road like Auntie Yomi, or houseboys and security guards. Mum and Dad still had to work hard. Dad was working in construction and Mum was doing secretarial work for him. We wondered what had happened to our home in South London and whether Dad had sold it. It just didn't make any sense to us why we'd gone from struggling in London to struggling in Lagos. However, in my family you didn't ask questions about money without being told to mind your own business. Which was weird because in this case it certainly seemed like it was our business.

Back at school, hardly any kids spoke to us for the first few weeks. Then one day another boy called us over. 'Hello dear!' he said to us. '*How you dey*? Come on! Come on! Do you know ten-ten?' We didn't know what he was talking about. 'Ah! What do they teach you in England if you don't know ten-ten? Here. I will teach you.'

Ten-ten is a simple hand-clapping game that everyone in Nigeria can play. It's basically a kind of superfast version of Pat-a-Cake. We'd noticed that all the students, both male and female, right the way up to the final year, played it all the time in classrooms and in the scrub outside that served as a playground. Stella and I had laughed to ourselves to see all these big bad Yoruba teenagers playing a game that, in my opinion, was reserved for little girls. This kid was called Sunday and when he offered to show us how to play the game we jumped at it.

He took us under his wing and it has to be said that Stella and I became the best at ten-ten in the whole year in no time at all.

'Ay! Ten-ten *balogun*! (Ten-ten warrior!)' shouted Sunday when we were going strong. Maybe it was because we were twins and in tune with each other but we could move our hands so fast that they were a blur to see. Ten-ten is a lot more complicated than Pat-a-Cake and you can play with two, three or more people and there are special hand signals that you can use to mean that you have to change players, touch the ground or freeze for a second. The trick is to make all the moves totally fluidly and you only lose if you miss a clap. Then you're out. The older kids even used to bet on this game.

Sunday was one of the unfortunate kids who had to stay in the boarding house all year long and he said, 'Stephen. It is a Godforsaken place. We have to get up at five o'clock to do chores. Sometimes they wake you with bells and sometimes they wake you with belts.' And of all the things that Nigerians could have kept up from the British, like healthcare or roads without potholes, they chose to keep prefects! Sunday would say, 'I miss my mummy and daddy. When they left me here I ran after them with tears in my eyes. "Please take me with you!" I shouted. Then last term, God bless them! They came to school and they showed off. Ah too much! They brought me pocket money but they put it in public eye. The prefects! They take my money.'

I'd never experienced the so-called Developing World and it was a shock to me that in some parts of Lagos there was no running water. However, when we told Sunday that we had a well in the back yard he was actually impressed! He asked us if he could come to our house to get water in the morning, as the public fountain was more than three miles away. When he came around, I brought him a bucket of water and he laughed at me because I carried it in front of me. 'Stephen! You need to learn bucket skills. You carry water like *oyimbo* (Westerner) and all the water is slopping out.

Here, put it on your head like this.' And he grabbed the bucket and balanced it on his head, moving skilfully from side to side to show me how it is done.

Next he showed me how to use a bowl to wash. 'First you put water, then you rub soap, then you rinse. In the boarding house, if you leave the water and go back to sleep, when you wake up, the water is gone. Then all you can do is rub and shine with Vaseline. You put on knees, elbows and lips to stop chaff.' As a kid from South London I'd only ever had to carry a bucket to mop the floor and Vaseline did not serve as a substitute for a hot shower in the mornings.

After a few months, we were beginning to feel like even if Nigeria wasn't the best place for us to be it was just a part of life to be dealt with. Sunday helped to defend us when the other kids made fun of us. He said, 'What you have to do is give them a knock on the head. Like this.' And he made a fist and hit me right on the skull. 'Yes! Now you can feel where your brain is in your skull. You can hit me back.' And he leaned forward and with a smile offered me his head to bash.

Nigerian students, even though they have to put up with all of this archaic discipline, or maybe because of it, are very well educated, especially in the sciences. Sunday was one of the smartest and he would even correct the teachers when they made mistakes. He thought it was very funny to expose their ignorance by using words they didn't understand. I remember one day when a teacher said to him, 'Sunday, you are more stupid than stupid.' He replied, 'Yes. But your medulla oblongata is very loose!' He really savoured the words – ME-DU-LLA OB-LON-GA-TA, which is a posh term for brains. If you hear it with a Nigerian accent then you can get the picture. Nigerian people will always surprise you. In the early days I needed to keep a dictionary handy at all times.

You really can never predict what a Nigerian will say, whether educated or not. Halfway through the term, the old auntie who ran the school kitchen said something that had Stella, Sunday and me in stitches. She had to quit her job to go and take care of her family in Benue State, which is in the middle of the country. Although the food she served was *terrible*, she was nice to the kids and we were sorry that she wasn't staying. We all asked her why she had to go. Without pausing and while still dishing out stew, she said, 'I must go back to Benue State immediately, my PLA-CEN-TA is buried there!' She made no attempt to explain what she was talking about, but we could work out that she meant her family were living there. *Medulla oblongata! Placenta!* Yoruba is a tonal language so it has a singsong quality. If you listen to how the Yoruba people speak, it really is a rich language to hear.

I reckon that Nigerians like sciences so much because they like the sounds of the long words more than anything else. Albert was always excellent at science and so he was getting along very well at school and was top of the class. To start with, he wasn't much happier than us because he was still horny as hell and wasn't getting any further with the girls in Nigeria than he had been getting with the girls back in the UK. But unlike in the UK, being at the top of the class actually makes you popular with the ladies in Lagos. Many Yoruba girls are a lot more religious and conservative than their English counterparts and so Albert, a sharp cookie, started to attend the local church group and soon he was getting dates left, right and centre.

So school was school, but at home Mum had just had carpets laid so we had to get used to the idea that we were really here for the long haul. I missed simple things from back home like watching *SuperTed* and *Danger Mouse* on telly on Saturday morning. The idea that I might never eat a Wham! bar again filled me with dread. Any last hopes that we harboured that this Nigerian holiday would be temporary went out the window. We had been deceived. Towards December, after we had been there about six months, I noticed that we had started to pick up Nigerian accents and I even started to pick up religion. Sort of. I started saying prayers every day in a little shrine that I built in my room with candles and a Bible. I prayed that we would be allowed to go back to London. I also decided that since God was so important here in Nigeria I'd pray to him to get good grades in the exams as opposed to taking the trouble to study hard. However, by the end of the school year in December, it appeared my prayers had not been answered. We were still in Nigeria, I failed all my exams and my shrine had mysteriously burned down.

5

THE CHRISTMAS HOLIDAYS WERE very welcome by the time they came in mid-December. We had a whole month off and the only thing I'd miss about school was Sunday. When I got my exam results, he was very concerned because I'd done so badly.

'Oh my God, Stephen! What will your parents say? You will be beaten! If you wake up it will be thanks only to God!'

He was very worried, because in Nigeria if you failed your exams you had to repeat the year, not just the exams. I swear there were people in the year above me who were thirty-five. Mum came into school and pleaded with the teachers. She said that it was unfair to penalize me as I had missed the first half of the year and they agreed to let me enter the second year. I'd thought that Mum and Dad would actually kill me, but once it was settled that I'd be able to move up to the next year they forgot all about it. They were very preoccupied with work at the time and were at least as eager for the holidays as we were.

Christmas and New Year are the biggest holidays in Nigeria and everyone goes back to their home towns and villages to spend time with extended family. So we all packed our bags, got in the van and headed for Abeokuta. We were going to stay with Mum's family because they had a huge house on the hill that could fit us all in. Mama Bunmi would go and stay with her daughter in a more modest apartment on the other side of town, but she made me promise that I'd come and see her in the New Year.

I asked her, 'Will you be coming to see us on Christmas?'

'Oh no, Stephen.' She smiled, kissed us all and walked quietly away.

'Dad? Why isn't Mama Bunmi coming with us?'

'It is because your mother's family go to church too much at Christmas time for her. She is more traditional.' Mama Bunmi had the tribal markings on her cheeks. She was an animist.

Abeokuta was only an hour and half north but it was very different from the hubbub of Lagos. Although it is the capital of Ogun State, it was still very rural and once we got there Dad had another hour of negotiating potholed dirt tracks to get to the house. The van itself was a novelty and loads of the local people followed us at walking pace as we wound our way through town. If any one of them had broken into a light jog they would have quickly overtaken us. In the end, it was good that we had attracted a crowd because once we got to the foot of the hill they helped us lug all of our bags to the house for a couple of naira each.

Dad warned us that although Mum's family were quite well off and had a big house none of them spoke any English at all. Not even Pidgin English. When we got to the gates Mum's mum, Mama Ola, ran to meet us. Her full name is Olatundun and it means in Yoruba 'tomorrow's wealth is sweet' and Granny Ola is one of the most hilariously bubbly and positive people who you will ever meet. She took an instant shine to us kids and, in full knowledge that we didn't understand much Yoruba, launched into endless enthusiastic conversations with us. When we looked at her with confusion on our faces, she just laughed, gave us little bits of sweet cake to eat with her fingers and pinched our cheeks.

The house we were to stay in was very odd to look at. It was the biggest in the area and sat on the side of a hill on two storeys, but it seemed a little bit like someone with a toilet fetish had built it. There were eight big bedrooms and all of them had en-suite bathrooms. There were two grand-looking living rooms with chandeliers, one on each floor, and they also came with toilets and showers attached. But the architect had neglected to realize that there is a limited water supply in that area of Abeokuta, so a huge tank had been installed and lorries would deliver fresh, clean water when it was needed. So to wash you still had to fill a plastic tub with water in the kitchen, carry it to the bathroom (whichever was closest), put it in the bath and sit in it using a smaller bowl to pour water onto yourself. Moreover, due to the unpredictable electricity supply, Mama Ola had to have a generator on the side of the house. However, it was normal to have it turned off when absolutely necessary. To us it just seemed hilarious that in this grand house full of chandeliers, everyone had to spend the whole time in the kitchen lit by battery-powered torches and lamps.

Over the course of a week a dozen or more relations turned up and the kitchen was definitely the centre of this travelling circus with Mamma Ola the ringmaster and cook. Christmas is a huge deal in Nigeria and you have to go to church not once but twice in the morning. The first time is to have a service and the second time is to sing carols and meet the neighbourhood. By the afternoon, two dozen people had settled into the house for the day and the adults were drinking Gulder beer with the kids getting high on sugary drinks.

Granny Ola had presents for all of us. She had selected a massive bolt of floral-patterned cloth, which in Yoruba is called *aso oke* (top cloth), and had new clothes made for everyone. It is very much in the Yoruba tradition to select a special cloth for family and friends to wear on special occasions. It's also about showing who's family and who's not. She demanded that we all wear the clothes straight away and with six people squeezed onto one sofa all dressed in the same floral pattern it was hard to see where one person ended and the other began. We looked like an amorphous Amos family blob with heads and hands appearing at random.

Stella and I were picked to help Granny in the kitchen and to start with it looked depressingly like it would be another meal made up of various kinds of paste. Stella was busy making the *garri* and I was helping to make *moin moin*, which is another kind of paste made from beans. Just as we were wondering if and when the meat was going to turn up . . . it did. On four legs. The butcher rounded the corner driving in front of him a fat goat with a bell around its neck and Mamma Ola got very excited and ran outside to greet him. She paid him the extra naira to kill the goat for us and a boy with a metal bath on his head grabbed the poor creature, stuck him in the bath and then stuck him for real. Half an hour later a skinned and gutted goat was sitting on the sideboard in the kitchen.

You can't be squeamish when it comes to food in Nigeria and Granny got out half a dozen different kinds of knife and set about chopping the animal into different cuts. There were steaks to barbecue, tough meat to stew, joints to roast, ears and cheeks to fry, trotters to boil into jelly and sweetbreads to be made. The kitchen became a carnival of energy and us kids were shooed away as the women set about preparing every part of the goat.

We enjoyed a banquet that day the likes of which I'd never had before or since. The men set about preparing outdoor tables and chairs and we all sat down. Dad dished out kola nuts to the adults as they waited. I think kola nuts should be called bitter nuts because to my palette they tasted so disgusting, but I found out they have caffeine in them and are good to eat if you are suffering from hunger pangs. As it happened, we didn't have to wait long for the food to start arriving. And once it started it didn't stop! Different dishes were ready at different times, so for hours and hours we all ate. First fried meats, then barbecued, then roasted, then stewed. The meal went on for so long that you could go to bed, sleep it off and then come back hours later to find a fresh plate in front of you.

The meal went on late into the night and by the next morning people were slumped on armchairs, across sofas, in beds and even outside at the dinner table. I thought back to the Christmases we hadn't really enjoyed in London. Christmas back there involved a roast in our jeans and T-shirts followed by watching telly and heading to bed at a sensible hour. By Boxing Day morning normally Mum or Dad would be back working and all memories of Christmas would be fading fast. Here in Abeokuta the mammoth task of cleaning up didn't even begin until Boxing Day evening, simply because it took that long to rouse everyone from their slumbers.

The next few days were marked by more relatives coming and going and, before we knew it, New Year's Eve had arrived. Nigerians know how to party like no others and that evening I was to learn the words *owambe* (party), *effizzy* (swagger) and *shakara* (showing off). Simply dressing for the occasion is an all-day thing for most women, who go out in their absolute finest. We all went out in the early evening wearing the clothes Mamma Ola had had made for us and the whole town was on the streets ambling around. There was to be a free party at the Abeokuta football stadium that night and, even though it was only a few minutes' walk, it took us nearly an hour to get there as we had to stop and talk to everyone that crossed our path.

Abeokuta stadium can hold 30,000 people in the stands, but when they open up the pitch for a public event it can hold twice that. As we stepped into the middle of the stadium we could have been a visiting football team dressed in our matching outfits. Massive petrol generators had been installed around the edges of the pitch and the sound they made was already deafening. Auntie Yomi from Ikeja had come up to Abeokuta from Lagos to set up the sound systems and when we arrived she came and greeted us one by one.

'Welcome! Welcome! It's loud isn't it? What a lot of work to control all of this! Thank God they chose some of us from Lagos to look after everything. But you wait until the *Gbedu* (sound systems) are installed. It's going to be a real *owambe* tonight!'

We watched all evening as people and equipment arrived. A small market was set up where people could buy food, drink, streamers, bangers and sparklers. When the massive sound systems were hooked up to the generators, they started playing music at a deafening volume and slowly more and more people from across town showed up. By nightfall, giant bonfires were lit all around the stadium and they served as little centres of activity, each with their own sound system playing different sorts of music from Afrobeat to soul and rap music. There was even one area in the stadium where they were playing church music and a gospel choir had turned up. Religion, as I said, is everywhere in Nigeria, but even if one person is very conservative and God-fearing they don't mind rubbing shoulders with people who are on the wilder side of life.

There were hundreds of *suya* spots, but instead of getting barbecue for us, Dad ordered the whole family a big bowl of pepper soup each. This is an incredibly spicy mixture that should have meat in it. Unfortunately, on this night they had substituted the beef for a piece of unappetizing cow skin, which floated around in the radioactively hot soup. Cow skin doesn't normally feature on the average Western menu. None of us could stomach it that night and we pushed it away. Aunti Yomi was surprised that we didn't take to it. 'Your English teeth cannot handle this delicacy,' she roared. 'Waste not, want not.' And she gathered all of our bowls together and ate every one, carefully chewing each piece of meat until the bowls were empty.

Mum and Dad had long since stopped listening to our complaints about the food in Nigeria. I had moaned to Mama Bunmi back in Lagos that I missed things like McDonald's and that unless you count puddings made from condensed milk there are almost no sweets available. When I explained to her about Wham! bars back in London she was disgusted and said, 'Ah, Stephen, if you have sweets all the time then you will die of piles!' She didn't mince her words.

I was hanging out by the sound system that was belting out Afrobeat music and a group of men in their twenties were standing nearby commenting on the women as they passed by. 'Look at her. Oh my God! *Shakara*! Plenty! Stop it, sista! I'm falling in love with you.' They noticed me watching them and they invited me to join them as they danced to the music. As we were dancing together, they offered me a sip of a milky-looking liquid in a clear plastic bottle. My taste buds were challenged once again: it had a weird tang. I didn't know it at the time but I was drinking palm wine, which is a wicked concoction made of fermented tree sap. It is a bit stronger than wine and after a couple of gulps I was feeling very weird, but it seemed to give me energy to dance more.

Soon I was sweating and had to stop. Needing a rest and with a woozy feeling in my head, I wanted to find the others. It was then that I saw the familiar brocade floral pattern and blindly stumbled over to a lady as she went to a different part of the stadium. When we got to another bonfire, I was starting to feel faint and I tugged on her sleeve. When she turned around I was horrified to see that this young woman was a total stranger. The cloth Granny had bought was obviously not that unique after all! I panicked. This was serious. I was in a stadium with tens of thousands of people around me, with barely adequate lighting, and I was lost.

The young woman must have seen fear rising in my face and tried to calm me down. With the music playing so loud she could barely hear me as I tried to tell her my name, but I think it was pretty clear that I was a lost kid: it's not like I was going to ask her to dance. She didn't worry at all and actually took a moment to find a handful of sparklers. She gave me one and took one for herself and once they were lit we waved them around in front of us to clear a path back to where the Afrobeat music was playing. It was actually kind of fun as we strode through the crowds waving the sparklers ahead of us.

'Not so fast, young man. Remember to walk with plenty of *effizzy*. You want people to stop and stare as you go past them. So remember to swagger.' I've never since managed a walk with such swagger and such fear hand in hand. I had no idea where my family was but somehow I knew that the feeling of being lost was nothing compared to the feeling of looking lost in a crowd full of people riding their *shakara* to the max.

After about forty minutes we were in a different part of the stadium and I heard a voice. 'Stephen! Stephen! Where are you?' Through my drunken haze, I was very pleased to see that it was Auntie Yomi. She was watching a group of teenagers who were having a break-dancing competition. I ran up to her and told her I'd gotten lost.

'Stephen! What is that smell on your breath?'

'Nothing.'

'You've been drinking toddy. What were you thinking?'

'I followed that woman!' Yomi looked up and saw the woman who was dressed in the same pattern as I was and she laughed.

'You had a lucky escape. But you won't be so lucky if your mummy and daddy find out you have been drinking! Look at you now. A big man! Well, you better steer clear of the others. Here come with me.' She led me to a *suya* stall, bought me something to eat and told me to wait there and not move an inch. She came back ten minutes later. 'There. I told them you are going to stay here with me and so they won't bother about you when they want to go home. We will have fun tonight. And don't go running off chasing women.' So I spent the rest of the night with Auntie Yomi and her DJ friends having a blast. She was so cool and full of life that to be honest I may have even had a few more mouthfuls of palm wine before the evening was out.

6

MUM'S FAMILY DIDN'T HAVE any electricity due to a corruption scandal, which meant that only half of the town got wired up. They were in the wrong half, but Mama Bunmi's daughter was in the right half. So even though they only had a small apartment they at least got to enjoy fans, lights and television. A few days into January, after everyone had got over the excesses of Christmas and New Year, I went to visit Mama Bunmi and she took me to see the sights of Abeokuta.

We visited the famous rock after which Abeokuta is named. Olumo Rock is a huge system of interlocking rocks and caves and it looks prehistoric, a bit like something out of *The Flintstones*. Abeokuta grew as a town because the surrounding villages were being pillaged for slaves by other tribes. People chose to live 'under the rock' because the rock and cave systems were easier to defend than the wide open plains surrounding it. We climbed the rock and, from that vantage point, we could see the first cathedral built in Nigeria, St Peter's Cathedral, and the other great building of Abeokuta – the Alake Palace, the home of the *Oba* (king).

Mama Bunmi may not have been as wealthy as Mum's family

but she was worldly and friendly and well connected. When we got to the Alake Palace this humble old woman went straight up to the guard on the door, curtsied, and asked right there to have an audience with the King. The guard laughed at her because she'd been there many times before and knew the King well. Nothing happens fast in Abeokuta and we were told that the King would see us in an hour but that until he was ready we were free to look around the palace.

Nigeria has a lot of kings and a lot of princes. Loads of Nigerian last names start with Ade-, which means 'king' or 'crown'. So if you know an 'Ade-something' then you know that they are descended from a king. That's not too difficult because in the olden days Nigerian *Oba* could have plenty of wives and plenty of children. If, when I say king, you start thinking of some kind of National Geographic-looking guy wearing leopard skin then forget it. This guy didn't have any real political power in Nigeria, but he was the most respected figure in the community, who wore tailored suits and had sent his son to be educated at Harrow.

The *Oba*'s palace is built in a very grand fashion. You go through a big archway into a courtyard with an east wing and a west wing. Mama Bunmi took me around the palace, which she obviously knew pretty well. The rooms were huge and, with their high ceilings, they kept cool in the tropical heat. It didn't look as if anyone lived there, but although the rooms were completely unfurnished, on every wall hung pieces of traditional West African art. Some were normal painted pictures, others were random bits of acacia and mahogany with burned-on etching. The King had plenty of wooden and iron sculptures and there were a lot of wood-carved masks with coloured material and feathers adorning them. There was one figure that seemed to be represented a lot. It looked like a huge spider. Sometimes the spider had a man's head or sometimes there would be a man riding on the back of the spider.

When the *Oba* came down to see us, he greeted Mama Bunmi warmly. He was wearing a linen shirt and trousers to combat the heat of the tropical midday and black leather shoes, but he wore a traditional round Nigerian *fila* cap on his head. He was very old but seemed to have lots of energy and he was so tall that he had to stoop to embrace Mama Bunmi properly. When I saw him, I prostrated fully on the ground as usual. He laughed at this and said, 'Ah! An *ajebo* who will prostrate to me!'

I winced at that. I still didn't like being called a butter eater at school.

When the *Oba* saw my reaction he said, 'Now, Stephen, seriously. Although you were born in the West, do you feel like a Nigerian?'

'Not really, sir.'

'Let me tell you something. You are Nigerian if you live in Nigeria. Even *oyimbo* can be a Nigerian, if he lives here.'

'Who is that man riding the spider in all of the pictures? Is it you?'

'Oh my God! No! That is a picture of Anansi the spider! Have you never heard of Anansi the spider?'

'I heard about him in school back in London – he's from Jamaica?'

The King kissed his teeth at that. 'From the Caribbean? Don't forget that here he born! Anansi is the number one trickster and joker in West Africa too. He can tell a tall tale to fool even a wise man. In fact he is the god of stories too. Don't you know any *anansesem*?'

The King took us from room to room and pointed out the spider in all of the different pictures. 'Each of these pictures tells an *anansesem*. An Anansi story. Look. That one tells how he became a spider in the first place.

'You see in the time *bifor bifor* the gods and men lived together on earth and no one did much and nothing much was going on. Anansi is a prankster and to relieve his boredom he played a joke on another god who didn't take it very well. You can see here Anansi is beaten and shattered into eight pieces but because he is a god he couldn't die, so he came back as a spider.

'Do you know how he got possession of the *anansesem* from his father, the king of the Gods?'

Mama Bunmi took over. 'The first myth of Anansi is how he got all of the stories from the king of the gods, who until then would always guard them jealously. Anansi boldly went up to his father and asked him straight, "Why do you keep all the stories to yourself? Give them to me."

'Anansi's father underestimated his son. He didn't realize that Anansi is a clever god who almost always gets what he wants. So he set Anansi an impossible task. The chief god said that he would give away all of the stories if Anansi could bring back to him four difficult-to-capture creatures alive: a lion, a whole nest of hornets, a python and Mmoatia, a demon.

'Anansi sat on the ground and thought to himself for a long time about how to go about getting these creatures to the chief god. The lion was a faster runner than Anansi even if he crawled on eight legs and he was bigger too, plus he had claws. Anansi could sneak up and try to bite him but then the lion might be killed. So he set about a trick. He knew where the lion's hut was and that he would go out hunting early in the morning and not come back until late in the evening, when he would be tired from all of his chasing and eating. So Anansi went to the lion's house in the morning and, once he saw lion run off, he used all of his legs to dig a deep hole in the ground. Once it was dug deep enough, he laid some palm leaves and twigs over the hole and sat back to wait.

'When the sun was going down that evening the lion came running back home and, just as Anansi hoped, he fell right down into the hole. Anansi crawled to the hole and said, "Ho! Lion! Are you stuck or something?"

'"Yes, Anansi, I fell in the hole. Can you help me?" Anansi went into the forest and found two sticks. He made a big show of reaching down to the lion with the sticks but lion's claws just slid right off of them.

'"How about if I dangle my web over the side and you can grab on to them and pull yourself up."

'"Yes. Yes. Send me down as many strands as you can."

'So Anansi let down as much web as he could and sure enough the lion eventually dragged himself back to the surface. When lion finally reached the lip of the hole he bolted for his front door, but he was so entwined in Anansi's web that he couldn't move an inch! He begged Anansi to let him go, but the wily spider knew that he had well and truly caught the lion and brought him straight to the chief god to get his reward.

'When it came to a whole nest of hornets it was a more difficult question. Hornets can't all be trapped in one place. What if just one escaped? Then the chief god would use it as an excuse to say Anansi had failed. He reasoned to himself that he would have to make them come to him willingly if he was to catch them at all. After thinking long and hard, Anansi decided to pick a gourd fruit from the forest. He ate the flesh to hollow it out and then filled the empty gourd with water. Next, Anansi scurried over to the hornets' nest and put a banana leaf on his head before emptying the gourd over himself and the hornets' nest at once. When the angry hornets came out to see what was going on, Anansi convinced them that it was raining and that they should shelter from the rain like he was doing with the banana leaf.

'"But how can we cut down a banana leaf? Let us use yours."

'"No. I need to use this leaf to shelter myself but here, I have this empty gourd, you can shelter in there if you want." The hornets thanked him and they flew one by one into the gourd and, once they were all in, what do you think Anansi did? Of course he sealed it up with the banana leaf and took the buzzing calabash filled with the gullible hornets back to his father.

'Next Anansi had to find a Mmoatia demon, which is a hard job in itself because they live in the hot lands of the north and don't like talking to strangers. Plus they can turn invisible and can even kill you if they just touch you. They are very dangerous creatures and not even gods like Anansi can get to speak to them. How could he catch a Mmoatia without being able to trick him with words? As Anansi travelled north he thought about it. Mmoatia are famous for two things. One is that they are very superstitious and they fear god. Number two is that they are greedy and can't get enough yams to eat. They like yams even more than the Igbo people down in the River States.

'When Anansi finally arrived at the Mmoatia lands he had come up with a clever plan. He went to the yam fields and he picked up three succulent yams, being very careful not to break the delicate tubers. Then he carved one yam very skilfully into an image of the chief god. He was a good craftsman with his eight legs and when he was finished he was happy with his work. He then coated the idol in a very thick and sticky gum that he got from a tree and placed it in a prominent position near to where the Mmoatia played. In front of the figure of the chief god he placed a wooden bowl and into it he laid the other two yams.

'Anansi watched from a distance as the first Mmoatia came by. He saw the yams and immediately set to devouring them. When he had eaten them and finished licking his lips, he prostrated in front of the idol to give thanks. But when he touched the yam carved to look like a god his hands stuck to it and stuck fast. With the Mmoatia's hands stuck to the yam husk, Anansi didn't have to worry about its death-bringing touch and had no trouble at all in carrying him to the chief god, who was getting worried by this time that he was going to lose his precious stories after all.

'The python is a wily and dangerous creature but Anansi knew his weakness. Python is proud and vain. All snakes are vain. That is why they change their skin every season to keep up with the latest fashion. Anansi went to see python and wondered aloud how long the longest snake is. Python slithered around Anansi and said, "Look at my beautiful body. I am the longest snake of all of them."

'"Yes. You are long but you are always coiled up and wound about yourself. How can I see how long you really are until you lie straight." So python tried to unravel himself, but he was so used to wrapping himself around things that he couldn't keep himself flat and straight on the ground.

'Anansi went to get a long branch from a tree. "Here, we can measure you against this." But when python tried to lie against it he couldn't stop himself from curling around the branch. You see every animal is a slave to his animal urges. "I know how to solve this problem," said Anansi. "I will tie your tail to one end of the branch and your head to the other and then we will know once and for all just how long your body is." The vain python was eager to prove that he was the longest snake and so he agreed immediately. Once the proud snake was safely tied to the branch all Anansi had to do was pick it up and take it to the chief god.

'When the king of the gods saw that Anansi had completed each of the four tasks successfully then he was forced to admit defeat. He relinquished all of the stories to Anansi who read them out loud for everyone to hear. That's why Anansi appears in so much art because the stories they tell are being told by him. Those are the stories we call *anansesem*.'

I looked wide-eyed at Mama Bunmi. I'd never heard a story like that at all. 'Stephen, close your mouth!'

'You are a Nigerian and so you should know some of our stories,' said the *Oba*. 'Just what are you learning in school?'

'Erm . . . agriculture and religious education.'

'Ah. Back-breaking labour. My own son is in England now and is exceedingly happy to forgo the plough. I'm sorry that you couldn't meet him. He is already preparing for the freezing spring term to start.'

'Stephen hasn't done well in school in Lagos. Now his sister is another matter.' I hated the way Mama Bunmi had said this. Adults seem to think nothing of making comments and shaming you in public. The whole notion of discretion is alien to them. Or at least it was to my grandmother.

'I understand, Stephen. It is hard for you to live in a foreign country away from your friends and family. You have the same problems in Lagos that my son has in England. You said that you don't feel Nigerian, but you have to embrace our culture. What are your parents teaching you?'

'They have concerns of their own at the moment. I tell you in Lagos *ground no level*.' Mama Bunmi meant that in Lagos times were tough.

'Stephen, what is your full name?' the *Oba* asked.

'Stephen Kehinde Amos.'

'So Kehinde means that you are the second born of twins. Amos and Stephen are good Bible names but you need a new Yoruba name now that you live here in Nigeria. Let me give you a present and you can say that you got it from the *Oba* of Ogun State.' He stood and looked at me for a moment and said, 'Since I am giving it to you in the hallway of my own palace I will give you the name "Afolabi" which means "born into high status" and the next time you see me you will call me uncle.'

Mama Bunmi looked very proud of me and, as we left, she curtsied low and I prostrated. So I had heard a story and been given a new name. Stephen Kehinde Afolabi Amos. It's just a name and it's not on my passport or anything, but it was a good present for an *ajebo* to get from a king.

7

WHEN WE WENT BACK to Lagos in January I felt a lot more at home and settled in Nigeria. The Christmas and New Year festivities had helped me slowly to adjust. I went back to school in the new year and when I saw Sunday I told him all about meeting the *Oba* and getting my new name.

'Ah yes. I've heard of him. You have been blessed! He is an educated somebody. And, Stephen, let me tell you I have heard some news. Everyone is talking about it. We are getting a new pupil this year. And this one is a real butter eater. He is an *oyimbo*.'

I had been in Nigeria for over six months and I suddenly realized that I hadn't seen even one white person in all of that time. I thought that if things had been tough for me then they were going to be really tough for him.

The kid was called Sebastien and his mum and dad were French and had come to Lagos to work in one of the oil ministries. He was older than us and was going into Albert's class. We all went up to him in break because we thought he would be desperate to make friends with another person who had lived in the West. He was just polite to us but nothing more and I was impressed that he seemed totally unfazed by the new school environment.

He was one of those odd kids that had lived all over the world. He was born in Kenya, had already gone to school in Hong Kong and New Zealand and didn't think much of being uprooted and set down in Nigeria. I had been moved around from school to school and home to home in the UK, but each and every time I had hated the change. However Sebastien took it all in his stride and he actually fitted in better than we had.

This *oyimbo* didn't mind it when the other kids walked past him in the corridors and brushed their hands through his long straight hair without even saying, 'Excuse me.' The kids were fascinated by this guy's hair because all of ours was cut very short. They said to him 'Ah. *Oyimbo*! He's not used to the barber.' They came up to him when he was eating and touched the freckles on his face and said, 'Ah. *Oyimbo*! He's not used to the bath.' One time the other kids said something that made Stella and I laugh. They came up to Sebastien and touched his nose. 'Ah. *Oyimbo*. He has a nose like an animal.'

'What animal?' said Sebastien.

'A nose like an elephant!' And everyone including Sebastien howled.

At the time a lot of Westerners were being brought into Nigeria to help regulate the oil supply because it was being badly mismanaged. In spite of the oil flowing freely from the Niger Delta, nobody seemed to be making any money from it. This was Nigeria in the mid-eighties during the rule of Ibrahim Babangida. This Babangida was a military ruler who had won power in a coup in 1985 from yet another military ruler called Buhari. Babangida was basically the most corrupt leader ever to rule in Nigeria. And that is saying a lot in a country where *chop I chop* (bribery and graft) was a national pastime.

When the British were in charge of Nigeria they took a lot of wealth from the country but they didn't sniff out the oil in the Niger Delta. After it was discovered in the seventies and eighties a lot of people like Babangida got very rich very quickly. They lost all control of themselves. There's a Pidgin phrase that people were using a lot at the time to refer to their leader and it goes like this: *Dat man na money miss road.* It means that someone who gets rich quickly doesn't know how to use it. In the case of Nigeria, the money missed the roads, missed the rail network, missed the hospitals, missed the schools, the courts and pretty much everything except the pockets of the generals.

Some strange things happened during this time. It is where the urban legend of the 53 suitcases comes from. In the eighties, the government noticed that millions and billions of naira cash was missing. So the President let everyone know that within a month he was going to revalue and change the currency so that all of the stolen naira would be made useless. Suddenly all the thieves who had salted the cash overseas got worried and tried to bring the money back into the country to exchange it. In a single day, two army officials were stopped at the airport coming into Nigeria carrying 53 suitcases full to the brim with notes. Nobody knows what happened to all the money that was stolen but it's clear to your average Nigerian that the money's not been spent on the country.

I don't mean to say that the Western companies managed to sort everything out or that they helped to put the oil revenue back in the hands of Nigerian people. Far from it. A bunch of multinational operators took control of the oil wells and they just stole all of the revenue for themselves. In 1980, Fela Kuti was so outraged by this that he wrote a piece of music about the shameful situation called 'International Thief Thief'.

'Many foreign companies dey Africa carry all our money and

go/ Them go write big English for newspaper, *dabaru* (spoil) we Africans.'

That was back in the eighties and you'd hope that things would have improved better today. But have they? In 2008, a brilliant Nigerian singer called Nneka released a tune called *Niger Delta* which says:

'Dem come fish our water empty/ Dem come *chop* our oil plenty/ Come take resources away/ Come take all of our riches.'

So in thirty years Nigerians have faced nothing but organized theft of their resources and what can the ordinary people do about it? They can fucking sing for it, that's what. In the words of Fela himself:

'Motherfuckers, bastard motherfuckers.'

So things weren't going too well for Nigerians as a whole and Dad was clearly having trouble making his construction business work. He would pay for materials and then they wouldn't arrive. He'd build a house only to be told once it was finished that the land belonged to someone else who was very happy to keep the house and not pay for it. There was one occasion when he tried to take the unscrupulous fraudster to court, but it didn't seem like a real court. It was more like a bribery bidding war and Dad didn't have the money to secure the right verdict.

Property fraud was so rife at this time in Lagos that signs started to appear on houses saying 'Not For Sale'. I asked Dad why anybody would put up a sign like that. He told me that it was because there was a new and innovative *chop* going around the city. In Lagos scam artists were selling people houses while the real owners were out at work. The scammers would pocket the cash and then when the new owners tried to move in they'd find that the house had never been on the market to begin with. This practice was becoming so prominent that people had taken to putting up signs to let everyone know that their homes were 'not for sale'.

When I told him that a white boy had come to school Dad reacted strangely. He started talking about how it had been growing up in Nigeria under British rule.

'Those white men. They came and cut up the land and they took gold home with them, but back then if you turned on the light it stayed on and if you bought a house it stayed yours. What is wrong with these greedy officials that just do what they like?'

With Dad's work drying up he didn't need a secretary any more and Mum began to stay home most of the time. It seemed like Mum and Dad were falling out of love with Nigeria and one day a huge argument erupted in the kitchen between Dad and Mama Bunmi. All we could hear was a lot of angry Yoruba language and the word 'Abeokuta' being said a lot. After a long time Mum went in and said, '*Abeg. Now make I hear word,*' and she took Mama Bunmi out with her and they didn't come back for hours.

The next morning Mama Bunmi went with us to school. She bought us breakfast, gave us all a big hug and told us that she was going home to Abeokuta. As usual nobody had bothered to ask us what we thought about her leaving. Once more the rug had been pulled out from under us kids. We were very sad to see her go and made such a big scene in front of the school that even Sunday came out to see what was up. When we told him that Mama Bunmi was going he cried too.

After Mama Bunmi had gone the house felt empty and to cheer us up Dad took the whole family to the National Theatre on Friday night for a street party. The theatre itself was rarely used, but there was always an *owambe* in the park in front of it at the weekend. We were all trying to forget about our worries by munching on *suya* and listening to the music when we saw Sebastien's family sitting at a table nearby. It wasn't hard to spot a white family in that situation. I called over to him and his mum and dad invited us to join their table; soon the grown-ups were all chatting together about the woes of Nigeria.

This party was not like the New Year's party in Abeokuta. In spite of the thousands of people and the sound systems breaking the decibel barrier, that *owambe* had been a friendly, family affair. This party was full of people drinking, hawking stuff and there was definitely a strange smell in the air. It was a bit threatening and I can tell you that I wouldn't have wanted to get lost there. I asked Sebastien what he thought about the diversity of people. 'Don't you find it very alien to you?'

'This is not diverse at all. In Hong Kong we saw Africans, Chinese people, Indians and white people. Everyone here is black. It's the least diverse place I've ever been to. Actually, it's boring.'

As he was saying the word 'boring' a dishevelled-looking woman came rushing past our table trying to hawk a bottle of some concoction. She shouted out, 'This tincture will cure your baldness, bring you good luck, it will help you keep your wife satisfied all night and keep you free of all diseases.'

We ignored her at first, but as she was moving away and fading into the crowd Dad called out after her, 'Ay, sista, *whetin dey happen?*'

The dishevelled-looking woman was Auntie Yomi! We hadn't seen her since Abeokuta when she'd been running sound systems at the party. At New Year's Eve she'd seemed larger than life and dressed to impress, but here she shrunk away from us when she saw her sister. She started to smooth her wrinkled linen shirt and pocketed the bottle. I remembered how she'd saved me from getting into serious trouble that night and I ran up to embrace her. She looked very embarrassed, but as far as I was concerned she was still the cool auntie and she gave me a big smile.

'Yomi, *kilode?*' What's wrong? asked Mum at first and then, 'What is in that bottle? What are you selling?'

Yomi came up to the table and waved a greeting to Sebastien's family. '*This?*! This is just rubbish but I have to try and sell them.'

'Come on, come on. I will buy one,' said Dad and passed over some naira without taking the bottle.

'Ah! Broda, *I tell you ground no level. Juss dey patch am.*' Things are tough. I'm just trying to survive. 'How you dey?'

'*Monkey dey work, baboon dey chop.*' One person toils, another enjoys the fruits of it.

She looked at the white family we were sitting with. '*Na go bye dat?*' Are you leaving?

'*Bodi no be firewood.*' A man can't work forever.

Mum looked guilty. 'Sista. I'm so sorry. I have not been in touch, but things have been so raw for us.'

'Jesus! For you and me too. Remember the Abeokuta *owambe?* They never paid me and I had all the expense of moving so many *gbedu* up there. I can't pay them, so now, the sound systems? They won't work with me. I can't get money. I can't get credit. They take *garri* from my mouth.'

In Nigeria there isn't any kind of welfare state and as Yomi had lost her income she'd had to sell her bungalow. She was now living in a tiny bedsit in one of the blocks in Ikeja.

'Why didn't you tell me you are in trouble? You will come and stay with us.'

'No! I'm telling you! My bungalow is gone but I have a place to live. I won't be a burden to you. If one finger brought oil it soiled the others.'

'Please. At least come and sit with us for a moment. Join us and have a drink,' said Sebastien's dad.

Yomi refused. 'Thank you, but I'm not finished. I'm not an old woman yet. The house sweeper's behind is never at one direction. I must work, work, work to get out of this and drinking Gulder beer will give me a headache. But ask me again another time and I will buy the drinks.'

Dad gave her some more money, but I knew that we were hurting for cash as well. I couldn't believe it. I couldn't believe that the woman who had welcomed us into the country with open arms was hurting so badly and that we were so powerless to help her. But, at the same time, I was impressed that she hadn't given in and let her situation get her down. She was still my cool auntie.

The next morning was a Saturday and we did what we always did on Saturdays, which was clean the house. But from the New Year, the government had passed a new law which Mum and Dad detested as another example of a lazy and corrupt administration. Every Saturday all residents on a street were forced to take part in something called Environmental Sanitation. This was essentially government-mandated chores. We had to collect the rubbish, sweep the streets and even try and fill the massive potholes with compressed garbage. I can tell you that you don't know what a waste of time really is until you are in an unpaved street with a broom, just sweeping dust. If we had swept until Monday all we would have achieved was to make a big hole in the ground, but in light of what we'd seen at the party the night before, we grumbled more quietly than normal.

Something definitely seemed to be up at home. During the following week, there were a lot of whispered conversations going on between Mum and Dad. We'd come back from school and things would be missing from the house. Slowly, all of Dad's equipment for work disappeared, then a wardrobe full of clothes would be gone. Normally, I would have rejoiced at the place being decluttered for once, but this time it all looked a bit ominous. Could we be so strapped for money that even the sale of Mum's sewing machine and her bolts of cloth would make a difference? We didn't get any explanations and we could see from Dad's face that we shouldn't ask.

That Friday night Mum made dinner for us on an outside barbecue. We'd been in Nigeria for almost a year by now and as there is no summer or winter out there, an outside barbecue is a good idea at any time. After we'd finished eating, Dad went to a box in the corner, fished out our passports and threw them on the kitchen table.

'We're going on holiday.' We all looked up when Dad said this. Another unplanned disruption was about to happen to us. I was not enthusiastic, but Stella reacted very differently and actually ran out onto the street. I ran after her.

'What's wrong, Stella?'

'Remember the last time we went on holiday?' she shouted with a whoop and a cheer. Could it be that we were going home to England? I quietly prayed that it might be, but with Dad you just could never tell. And you could never ask either.

Once more we had to pack up the entire house and we loaded the rusty van to the brim. We still hadn't been told where we were going and when we reached Lagos airport we just followed Dad, carrying boxes and bags in our hands like a family of displaced ducklings. In the year we had been in Nigeria, West African Airways had shut down and Dad marched us to the British Airways ticket booth. My heart was thudding in my chest as Dad picked up seven one-way tickets to London. Stella nearly dropped the box she was holding she was so happy.

As the plane took off, Albert, Stella and I felt good: we'd arrived on an African carrier to live an African life; now we were going home on British Airways to resume our British lives. But who knew how long this would last? The flight was completely different from the one we'd taken over to Lagos a year before. There were films to watch on this plane. There were stewardesses that served us hot English food. As we looked out of the window all we could see below us were fluffy clouds flying past, looking deceptively solid. I sat in my seat and thought about how only the week before I had been sweeping a dusty Lagosian street and playing ten-ten with Sunday.

I suddenly felt very angry. Although I was happy to be going home, why did it always have to be so last minute and why were we never told anything beforehand? I never got to say goodbye to Sunday or to Mama Bunmi. I didn't even have their addresses if I wanted to write to them. What about the *Oba* of Abeokuta? Would I never see him again? Would I never get to meet his son? And Auntie Yomi too? Dad was constantly uprooting us and, as I heard our hand luggage bumping around in the overhead locker, I thought, We are just pieces of luggage to pack up and move about.

Though there was undoubtedly much love and care in my family, talking about our feelings was basically absent from our lives. I have no idea if this is a phenomenon of every large family, but in a way I can understand it. Keeping five kids safe and healthy is a big enough job; worrying about their mental well being too would keep Dr Freud busy for months. Only later on in my life did I begin to appreciate the trials and tribulations my parents must have gone through. I'm sure there was a lot of personal stuff they didn't or couldn't share with us and, ultimately, I know that they sacrificed a lot for us.

It's no surprise that these days some of my friends describe me as being a bit secretive. The thought of opening up and being emotional will never be something that comes naturally. What makes it easier is when I see how some of my closest friends have a completely different relationship with their families. My friend Dustin is so close and open with his parents and siblings that I sometimes feel I'm watching an episode of *The Brady Bunch*. It's bewildering to see him argue, discuss and make up with his family all in the space of minutes. I'd rather not get involved in that kind of drama. Some people might disagree, but, in my case, 'avoiding the issue' are words to live by.

When we arrived in London the first thing we did was open up our bags and pile on as many clothes as would fit on our bodies. We had brought so much stuff with us that Mum had to take a taxi by herself and we stuffed the cab full of bags and boxes after she got in. Dad took me and the rest of the kids on the Tube. Cordelia and Chris, who were now five and six years old, were excited to take an Underground train as they simply couldn't remember having used the Tube before. About halfway down the Piccadilly line a large Jamaican woman got on the Underground. She was standing opposite, watching us kids as we sweated, each wearing three T-shirts, three jumpers and our feet swelled with the many pairs of socks we'd pulled on. She was laughing to herself at the sight when a foul smell pervaded the Tube. Someone had farted. She looked at us and smelled the air tilting her head upwards. Then she started moving her mouth. Like she was eating it. And declared in a thick accent, 'Cha! Somebody bottom dirty!' We all screeched with laughter.

Changing onto the Northern Line we eventually arrived at Tooting Tube station. We emerged onto the street and found our way to the tiny flat that Dad had got for us on Fountain Road. It was a dodgy-looking block and had only three bedrooms for Mum and Dad and the five of us kids, but we didn't mind the cramped conditions because we felt like we had finally come back home.

Once more the exhaustion of the trip was overridden by the excitement of arriving in a new place and I resolved to do something I'd missed for the whole previous year. I took a pound from Dad and went out to buy junk food. I was still only twelve years old and Woolworth's Pic 'n' Mix was calling out to me. Tooting is a hugely Asian area and I was amazed to see so many Indian people out and about after a year of seeing only black faces. I passed temples, mosques and loads of Indian sweet shops. I was so busy staring that I almost ran straight into a little old Indian woman who scowled at me.

'Don't you know your shoe is untied?'

I could never understand old people's paranoia about untied shoes. It's as if having a lace flying about is as likely to result in a broken neck as having a noose looped around your head while standing on a rickety ladder. I just looked at her and right there on Tooting High Street she got down on her knees and tied up my shoelaces for me, before getting up, smiling at me and tottering off. I have to tell you that after coming from Nigeria where I'd had to spend half my life on my knees or on my belly prostrating to strangers this was a wildly different experience.

In Woolworths a Chinese man served me two Wham! bars almost without looking up and, as I left the shop, one was already in my mouth. I remembered how much Stella liked sausage rolls – another treat long denied us in Africa – so I headed into a bakery on the way back home. I had just enough money to buy a roll from the white woman behind the counter and, as she handed it over, she said with a wink, 'There you go, lover. They put the bollocks and everything in that.' I was truly home!

As I walked the rest of the way back to Fountain Road with the warm sausage roll turning the paper bag see-through with grease in my pocket, I realized that in the space of ten minutes I'd come into contact with three different people from three different races: a trip to the shops in London does more for racial relations than any Benetton advertising campaign can ever hope to achieve. Forget trying to fit in if nobody else bothers with it. I wasn't a Lagosian or a Londoner. I was just myself, and realizing that, I walked down the street that night with a little bit more *effizzy* in my step.

8

COMING BACK TO ENGLAND was a real shock to the system. We'd missed a whole school year and were going to enrol in secondary school a year late. We were up to scratch in most of the academic subjects, but we were going to have to unlearn such a lot of habits that we'd picked up in Nigeria. School started two hours later over here; agriculture and RE were out the window. Making your own uniform wouldn't be seen as a badge of honour in London and we went out to buy cheap polyester uniforms off the peg from Marks and Spencer.

The teachers had been disarmed and we could get away with a lot more, which was good. But we had to deal with another kind of torture when we finally enrolled, because to my horror, Stella and I were separated into different classes. There was a policy back then to separate twins from each other as soon as possible. It's the kind of wrong-headed nonsense that no one in Nigeria would ever think of bothering with. We only got to see each other at lunch breaks when we'd play ten-ten and go out to buy crisps from the local newsagent.

Thankfully, these days that policy has been reversed. Basically, schools have changed for the better since the eighties, although I saw my nephew recently and he said that kids today aren't allowed off school grounds at any time during the day. Apparently, people are worried that paedophiles are lurking behind every corner, which is ironic because back then half of our teachers were seriously pervy. I remember we had one teacher who would just wander around the boys' changing rooms making sure everyone was showering naked. He didn't even teach PE. And if we forgot our kit? You guessed it! We had to do it in our vest and pants. Even the cross-country run! Although to be fair we lived in South London and if you were a thirteen-year-old boy out on my local high street in just your vest and pants then you'd better be running. This was considered normal back then. It was so ridiculous at my school that the register should have been a list of all the teachers who would qualify as a sex offender today.

So at the age of thirteen I was thrown into a new secondary school without my trusty partner in crime and it was awful. I wasn't particularly academic and I wasn't sporty either, much to my teachers' confusion. When you're a black kid at an all-white school and you're not sporty, people start to think you must be adopted. I hated all the different games we had to play and I still can't swim properly. When we had swimming classes I used to just walk along the bottom. What can I say? The afro and water are like a jockey's left and right testicle. They're never going to meet.

Without Stella, I was literally the only black kid in class. And so yes, I started to act out, a lot. I think it was the culture shock of coming from a country where you could get beaten with a two by four for looking at the teacher wrong. When you're used to seeing that sort of thing, being threatened with detention or writing lines just doesn't carry so much weight. Suddenly, I could get away with anything and I used to really push my luck. I would always be caught talking in class. I remember one time my English teacher

Miss Matthews said, 'Stephen! Please put your hand up if you want to talk!' and I said, 'I didn't know we had that kind of relationship, miss.' Yes, a precocious bastard was I. And I used to come up with nicknames for all the kids in the class and the teachers too. Although a joker, I still wasn't popular at all. In fact there were only three people in class less popular than me: Cindy (who I christened 'Four-eyes'), Aled ('Potato Head') and Gary ('Smelly Git'). I wonder why no one liked me?

And then there was Dustin. He was small for his age and he had bad asthma so he was off sick a lot. I didn't tease him because he was one of those people that just managed to fade into the background. Like me, he was unpopular, but, whereas I tried to be the centre of attention, he just wanted to be left alone and, using some kind of instinctive camouflage technique, for the most part, he was. He sat at the back of the class like me and he laughed at all my jokes although we weren't exactly friends.

There was one teacher that really, really hated me. Mr Hackett was his name and he taught maths. He would scream at us until he was literally blue in the face. Plus he had a huge head, way too big for his body, and the reason he really hated me is because I'd given him a nickname that had stuck. With his huge head that regularly turned blue with rage I'd taken to calling him 'Moon Face'. Dustin particularly liked this nickname I gave him because Mr Hackett was always making fun of Dustin and used to call him 'Shorty' and 'Chicken Legs'. That teacher was a bully, pure and simple.

As is always the case, one day I was right in the middle of the classroom making fun of him when he walked into the room. The whole class was looking at me and laughing their heads off as I chanted, 'Moon Face! Moon Face!' There was a big pillar in the middle of the classroom and I was poking my head from one side to the other 'Now you see him . . . Whoops! You still do!' I was having a great time when a deathly hush came over the whole room. I should have clocked something was wrong but I kept on going 'Now you see him . . .' And there he was, right on cue. His big blue moon face screaming at me to sit down. He really let me have it and I was in detention for a week.

From then on, he was a total sadist to me. He'd read out my homework when it was wrong and if he noticed I wasn't paying attention to him (which was often) he'd make me come up to the blackboard to do a sum that was totally beyond me just to humiliate me. And then there was one day he really pulled a number that I'll never forget. When I was a kid I was a sweet addict. I'd load up on Coca-Cola and pop Wham! bars like they were crack cocaine. In break I'd be at the vending machines getting my usual fix and one day I'd drank too much pop and was busting for a pee right in the middle of his lesson. I raised my hand and asked him if I could go to the toilet, but he said no. I was getting really desperate and so I asked him again, but he told me I'd have to wait with an evil little gleam in his eye.

There I was, squirming in my seat, absolutely desperate for the loo and, you guessed it, I couldn't hold it any more. I bolted out of the classroom with 'Amos! Amos! Get back in your seat!' ringing in my ears.

I didn't quite make it. Five minutes later, I returned to class, panic stricken and rather sheepishly holding a poster for the debating society over my trousers.

'How dare you! Where have you been? You need permission to leave my classroom. Come to the front of the class!' He pointed at me. 'I'm going to make things really difficult for you, Amos! You're a troublemaker. I think that's another detention for you. And what's that you've got there?'

'Nothing, sir.' By this time, I was really sweating, hoping he'd let me just sit down. But he didn't. Right there at the front of the class, he ripped away the poster and there, exposed for all to see, was a wet patch in the front of my trousers.

'Sir! Sir! Stephen's wet himself,' screamed four-eyed Cindy, and all the kids turned to me and laughed. Today, although I can't really remember their faces and I can't really remember their names, I can sure remember their pointing fingers and their horrible laughter. It was the most humiliating day of my life and I ran straight home.

When my mum saw me she was horrified. Less because of what had happened and more because I'd ruined my uniform. The next day she went marching to the headmaster to complain and Mr Hackett and I became firm enemies. A line had been drawn in the sand and I swore I'd get him back one day.

At the back of our classroom on the side nearest the window was a big supply closet that contained the chalk, the board rubbers, the dictionaries and all the usual stuff that a school needs. It had a lock but the key wasn't very well guarded since no one was going to steal dog-eared old dictionaries. In fact the classroom monitor, who was just another kid, was normally asked to go and fetch stuff for the different classes, so we all knew that the key was kept in the top drawer of the teacher's desk. So, one day, a few weeks later, once the whole pant-wetting incident had blown over, Dustin and I decided to teach Mr Hackett a lesson.

Every morning once the roll was called, the attendance sheet sat on the front desk for the rest of the day so that the teachers could check that all the pupils that had come to school were in all the classes. No teacher wanted a kid to play truant, especially not a monster like Mr Hackett who knew that every student in class would have given anything to get out of an hour of his company.

So we made up our minds to have a little bit of fun with him and see if we could get the upper hand for once. Mr Hackett already hated Dustin and me the most in class, so what was the worst that could happen if it all went wrong? In Nigeria that's the kind of question you wouldn't want to think about but this was a different world.

During break time, I sneaked the key to the supply closet from the teacher's desk, unlocked the door and pocketed the key. When the bell rang for maths class, Dustin, who was about a foot shorter than everyone else in class, hid under some coats behind my chair at the back of the classroom. Sure enough, Mr Hackett checked the roll and immediately noticed that Dustin was missing.

'Where is that Dustin? Who's seen Dustin?'

'Maybe he's still out in the playground, sir,' said suck-up four-eyed Cindy.

'That sickly weasel?' Mr Hackett liked to pick on Dustin because he thought that he was weak and easy game. 'Dustin! You don't want to play games with me!' he shouted at no one in particular and everyone at the same time. His face was already getting that bluish tint.

'He's hiding in the cupboard, sir!' I shouted out.

'I bet you think this is very funny, Amos! Well, you'll be laughing out of the other side of your face!' Mr Hackett was already striding as fast as his little legs could carry him to the back of the room, his head wobbling and his mouth revving up for the abuse he was about to dish out.

'What did I do, sir?' I stood up and held up my hands innocently as he pounded past me.

'Sit down!' He threw open the door. 'DUSTIN!'

I ran behind Mr Hackett and pushed as hard as I could on the small of his back and he sprawled into the closet. I slammed the door shut and, although my hands were shaking a bit, I managed to lock it from the outside before he could get up and turn around. I couldn't believe what I'd done.

I turned to the whole class who were staring at me with open mouths and for a split second they could have turned against me. Then Dustin launched out of the coats at the back of the room and hollered. 'Whoooop whooop! Yeeeaahhh!' he screamed out and suddenly everyone else joined in. It was like all hell had been let loose in that classroom with the kids dancing around the aisles in between their desks and chucking their pens and papers everywhere.

Mr Hackett was banging on the door and shouting at the top of his lungs from inside the closet and so we just whooped louder and banged our desk lids up and down and all the while Dustin was clutching his stomach with laughter. The louder Mr Hackett banged the louder we shouted and I was strutting around at the front of the class shouting, 'Moon Face! Moon Face!' at the top of my lungs. It seemed like ages but probably only lasted about five minutes, and I was doing my 'Now you see him . . . Whoops you still do,' when the head teacher walked in through the classroom door.

'What's going on in here?' demanded the head to a roomful of ashen-faced and deathly quiet pupils. Suddenly, all we could hear was the banging from the supply closet and the cries of Mr Hackett.

'Let me out, you little shits! You're going to be in so much trouble now.' The head teacher ran to the back of the room, found the key in the lock where I'd left it, opened the door and Mr Hackett's giant blue face came out of the closet door hyper-ventilating with rage.

All the pupils were in shock, except for Dustin who was still clutching himself with laughter. Mr Hackett couldn't contain himself and, quick as a flash, ran over to Dustin who was now in a heap on the floor. 'What's so funny? What's so funny, you little shit?' he screeched.

Dustin still didn't get up and he was really clutching himself hard now and going a bit blue himself with the strain of it all. I thought he had better get his giggles under control. Mr Hackett grabbed him from up off the floor by his shoulders and pushed him up against the wall, but Dustin still couldn't catch his breath.

'I'll show you!' screamed Mr Hackett, but by now we could see something was wrong and Dustin's eyes were popping bloodshot out of his head and he was grabbing at his own throat.

Mr Hackett was still pushing Dustin up against the wall and shouting into his face when the head teacher barged him out of the way. 'Mr Hackett! Put him down!' Dustin collapsed to the floor still clutching at his chest and throat.

'He's having an asthma attack!' screamed out Cindy hysterically. Mr Hackett's jaw dropped open.

'Don't just stand there! Get the nurse!' shouted the head teacher to Cindy, who ran out of the room as quickly as possible.

They had to call an ambulance to the school, and if there's one thing teachers hate more than kids who play truant, it's kids who are dying on their watch. That day the maths class was dismissed early.

I thought I was going to get expelled, shopped to the police straight away or worse, for starting the whole thing. I was terrified of what my parents were going to say and I was really worried about Dustin too. Instead, something weird happened. It turns out that when the life of a pupil is hanging in the balance suddenly that pupil is elevated from being just a sickly kid and becomes an actual human being. I hardly got into any trouble at all once it was clear that Dustin was going to be OK and came back to school. The rest of the kids, who'd been given a little taste of freedom from the tyranny of teachers, were vague about the details of the whole incident in the way that kids can be.

And Mr Hackett, rather than blaming me for the whole thing, focused his time on claiming to be seriously claustrophobic. Pathetically, he tried to explain that he'd suffered a psychotic moment of madness and that's why he'd been manhandling and screaming at a little boy who was about an inch from suffocating.

Mr Hackett got fired from the school within a week. The kids in class were so grateful to Dustin and me for getting rid of the hated maths teacher that they actually started being nice to us and, most importantly, Dustin and I became best friends. We said to each other seriously a few weeks later that if only we'd known beforehand that Mr Hackett was badly claustrophobic, well, we would have played the prank a whole lot sooner.

Weirdly, I saw Mr Hackett again about a decade later in a gay club, waggling his head from side to side and making eyes at anyone who'd look his way. I avoided eye contact. So it looks like that particular incident wasn't the first time that he'd been stuck in a closet after all. Maybe it goes some way towards explaining why he'd been so bad-tempered as a teacher. Hey! The life of a closeted gay maths teacher with claustrophobia can't be easy, but he didn't have to take it out on us.

9

After coming back to London, my family settled down around Tooting in South London. We still moved houses a lot but basically stayed in the same area, moving a few stops either up or down Zone 3 of the Underground's nefarious Northern Line. Tooting is full of weird and wonderful characters and soon people-watching became my number one pastime. You can't help absorbing things from your surroundings and I may have been born with funny bones, but around where I grew up there were a lot of funny people. Now when I say funny, I don't mean Noël Coward funny or even Jimmy Tarbuck funny – I mean funny like a Grace Jones in her 'I'm Andy Warhol's muse and like to eat live babies' phase.

There was the mad old lady who lived in a bush, shouting to herself and to passers-by who got too close. Maybe she lived in a bush because she wanted privacy, but it was hard to avoid her because dressed in formless rags and complete with unkempt sticking-out hair she blended into the bush perfectly. You could be wandering happily down the street whistling to yourself without a care in the world when suddenly you'd catch a glimpse of rustling leaves in the corner of your eye and the next thing you knew the bush would start screaming gibberish at you. I could have given Usain Bolt a run for his money on more than one occasion after running into her.

Then there was the weird man who wore a bicycle helmet covered in little multicoloured fairy lights. This mad genius had actually rigged his bicycle with a generator that powered the lights when he pedalled. I thought he looked very festive, like a kind of homeless Father Christmas. Except he didn't have any presents to speak of except for a can of Special Brew and a mangy dog on a rope and you definitely wouldn't want to sit on his knee.

The White Lady was a pretty amazing sight to see. She was in fact a totally respectable black woman, but the odd thing about her was that she wrapped her entire body from top to toe in glisteningly clean white cloth and she bound her hair in the same white material. Not only that but she painted her face and hands with white make-up. What surprised me was the fact that she seemed to have plenty of friends who'd stop and chat to her completely normally and without saying things like 'Are you mental or what?' She looked like a tall, slender, very much alive Egyptian mummy.

The White Lady originally hailed from Nigeria and so, in spite of her odd looks, Mum got to know her very well. Also Mum was working as an Avon lady at the time and so it made sense for her to get to know this woman who clearly had a need to buy large amounts of make-up. Apparently something had happened to her during the Biafran civil war in Nigeria that had badly damaged her and she'd fled to London. I could always tell when the White Lady was visiting because Mum would put an extra layer of protective plastic sheeting on all the furniture (she put protective covers on everything anyway as a matter of course). Nobody would ever accuse Mum of being overly sentimental and when the White Lady left our flat she would say that it was a shame to see a young woman end up this way but 'How can she have enough time on her hands to be able to get ready like that every morning? That sista is of *one kind* (odd). It's because she has no issue! And think of the cleaning bills!'

I think it's possible there was some chemical in the water supply in Tooting that was making people act strangely and it was no surprise to me that the biggest mental institution in South London was at the top of a big leafy hill round the corner from where we lived. A mental institution with a big outpatient clinic. The local shopkeepers were used to people with bad Tourette's coming into the shops to buy a bunch of bananas while barking at them like a dog. Some of these characters were probably patients out for a stroll but the rest of them just felt at home in this environment and gravitated towards the area. This was care in the community before there was a government policy on care in the community.

There was one old Caribbean guy who was my favourite of the whole mad lot. He was teetering somewhere between insane, eccentric and just plain old. Mad Marvin or Marvin the Menace, as the local kids called him. He would always wear the same tattered old jumper and raggedy shorts even in the dead of winter and you'd see him out all the time because he had about a hundred dogs. He'd walk them in the local park a dozen at a time. They were completely wild and would try and chase after the boys as they rode their bikes shouting, 'Oi! Marvin the Menace!' The kids didn't have much to worry about as most of the dogs had only three legs. He had come to live in London in the fities because his dad had fought for the British in World War II. If I thought things were tough for black people in the seventies and eighties, it was nothing compared to the abuse he'd suffered and it had unhinged him pretty badly.

He was funny and he did funny things. Like one time he was arrested on the open-air top deck of a double-decker bus for lighting a Bunsen burner. When the police got him he said, 'All me want is a cup of tea a' door', before presenting them with a tea bag, mug and billycan. He told me later, 'Stephen, the judge was a fair man. He said "Sir, nex' time you want a drink o' tea on a bus make some before you go out and keep it in a Thermos", before he show me his Thermos that he keep himself behind the judge's desk! An' they let me off wit' a warning. Ha!'

Marvin didn't have much, but he did live in a big house at the bottom of the hill, which he said his mum and dad had left him when they died. Whether that was true or not was highly debatable because Dad told me that all the houses in that row were squats and that I shouldn't hang around down there. Marvin was always worried that the authorities would take his house away from him. He'd say: 'I'm getting to be ageable. Them dogheart man wait till I lose the last marble in my head and I'll end up in that hospital up the road with the rest of them.'

With all of these unique individuals in the neighbourhood there was always someone to pass the time of day with. You couldn't leave your doors unlocked or anything, but there was a sort of community spirit and so people noticed when, one day, a truly weird and highly scratty white man turned up and started to hang around with Marvin. This guy scared all the kids because, bizarrely, he had no lower jawbone at all. I don't know if he'd lost it in an accident or was born that way but he looked very strange and when he talked his lower lip vibrated weirdly and he spat. He was always hanging around Marvin and so everyone began to avoid both of them in the park.

Marvin didn't seem happy to have this new companion and

after a while even my dad noticed that he was looking very down and so one day we finally asked him what was going on. He cried out to us, 'That man jus' won't leave me alone! Him say that it be his house that I've been living in all these years. He took me front door key, copied it and now he won' go away.' He looked up to my dad and quietly added, 'An' him kick the dogs.' Dad, being Nigerian, had a lot of respect for his elders and even though Marvin wasn't playing with a full deck of cards it broke Dad's heart to see him brought so low.

Since moving back from Nigeria some subtle changes had come over my whole family. The challenges that we'd faced there made any difficulties we encountered here in the UK seem much more manageable. Stella and I had become a lot more confident in dealing with the other kids at school and Dad had relaunched his construction business in London with gusto. We were still living with far too many kids (and Mum was pregnant again!) in a small flat, but money wasn't as tight as it had been in Africa. Dad's hard work was paying off and his self-esteem rose in line with his earnings. In the past he would have just stayed well out of the affairs of local people but now he confronted this jawless white man in the park that same day.

'What are you doing tormenting an old man? You should be ashamed of yourself. Why don't you take yourself away from here before I call the police?'

Although the interloper cringed visibly at being challenged by Dad, he frothily lisped back, 'Call the polithe then. What will they do, ey? I can live here ith I want to. Mind your own buthineth. That house ith too big thor an old man anyway. He jutht wants it thor himself. He shouldn't be there. He thtole it.'

To which Marvin cried, 'No! You vex me now. Me know meself. Me no tief. Don' accuse me!' He was clearly getting very upset and feeling very helpless in light of this scary-looking white man.

'Well pwoove it then. You can't!' And Jawless went back to the big house trying to act as if nothing had happened, leaving poor Marvin sitting on the park bench taking comfort from the six or seven dogs he'd brought with him that day.

That evening my dad complained to Mum. 'It's just not right for Marvin to have to put up with this greedy intruder. He's too old to handle this himself.'

'If it's his house why doesn't he just call the police and be done with it?' Mum was always reasonable in a crisis.

'Most of those houses down there at the bottom of the hill are just squats. Who knows who really owns them? If Marvin ever had any documents to prove it's his I'm sure he's lost them by now. And if he calls the police or the council they'll probably repossess the whole lot anyway and he'll be totally homeless.'

'Why are you getting involved in his business anyway? He's a grown man. And a Caribbean at that,' piped up the White Lady who was pawing through a catalogue of Crystal White cosmetics my mum had laid out for her. 'Can't he act for his own best interests?'

'He must be seventy years old and you know he's not all there upstairs. No! An old man is there to talk. His days for action are long passed. What muscles can he flex around this bully? Imagine spending your final years being pushed around by a jawless white man. Something must be done.'

And so Mum put on a pot of coffee and the three of them set to it. 'So, we can't call the police or the council?' said the White Lady. 'And we can't just magic this white man away. Maybe I should sneak up behind him and say boo! Give him the fright of his life!' She cackled and everyone in the room turned to her at once. If she hadn't been sitting on the sofa in our living room with a cup of coffee on her white-painted hands it might have been quite frightening. This apparition in white did indeed cut a ghostly figure.

'This man is a coward of the worst kind. Abusing a defenceless old man. His fear can be his undoing,' said Dad as he sipped his coffee. 'Let us find out a little more about our unwanted neighbour and see if we can't spook him right out of the borough.'

The White Lady smiled back at him and said, 'I suppose I can make some enquiries.'

So over the next couple of weeks, the White Lady launched a surreptitious investigation into the troublesome intruder. I often saw her chatting away to the neighbourhood eccentrics who, though a little on the weird side (to put it mildly), were best placed to see his comings and goings. It's true to say that it's the street spooks who are the experts on the local community. They know which marriages are failing. They know which kids are out buying drugs on street corners. They know who's going out of business. All the life that we ignore as we're rushing about living our lives is noticed by these people and they took a special interest in Marvin; he was one of them, after all.

To no one's surprise, the White Lady found out that Jawless was without any friends and was a total lowlife sponger. He never bought food and always took half of Marvin's sandwiches when they were in the park together. He was afraid of the dogs and would have got rid of them if Marvin hadn't defended them like they were his own children. And Dad learned that he liked to drink in the local pub every Tuesday, Thursday and Sunday, where he would sip his beer disgustingly through a straw in the corner. Dad came home and tried to mime this to us by pulling a hilarious face and using many horrible slurping sounds. Mum said that he was mad to get involved in the business of a *were* but she couldn't help laughing a little bit too.

One Saturday morning not long afterwards, Dad and I were in the park when the White Lady came up to us and whispered something to Dad that made him laugh heartily. He followed her to a bush where he talked with Marvin and the bicycle-helmeted man (complete with dog on rope). The bush they stood next to would give the occasional shake and so I figured the bush woman was involved in the conversation too. When Dad came back to where I was playing, he smiled and said, 'Stephen! You just watch. Tomorrow we will put that evil interloper under heavy manners!'

The next day Dad was strangely excited and at about ten o'clock at night Marvin came around to the back of the flat with two of his least mangy dogs. In fact they were pretty energetic and were barking all over the place. When Mum heard all the commotion she came out the back and screamed, 'Get those dogs away from here.'

'Hello, Mrs Amos,' said Marvin with a nervous smile.

'*Ifemi*, I told you Marvin was coming around.'

'He'd better not leave them here. Don't call me *ifemi*! You are mad if you think this will work! *Were*! When is this all going to be over?'

'Shortly my dear,' said Dad. 'Stephen and I will take these animals for a walk. Come on! Come on!' He turned to me. '*Put leg for road.*'

'Don't be long! Stephen has to be in school tomorrow morning and you need to work unless you want to lose your job and join those *were* people in the park for good!'

Dad gave me both of the dog leads and we walked back towards the park with Marvin hurrying ahead to his house. I have always loved animals but these two were quite a handful to control and when we got to the park I asked Dad, 'What's going on?'

'Quiet, Stephen. It's on a strictly need-to-know basis.' The park ran the whole way down the hill and from the entrance nearest the bottom we could just make out the entrance to Marvin's house.

Even though it was a squat it was one of those very dilapidated old Georgian townhouses that you used to find all over South London. You could tell that it had once been a very posh building and it was four storeys tall, with a gate leading through a wildly overgrown front garden to a grand old porch, complete with porch light. I had been inside before and it totally stank of dog, was falling down and only had an outside toilet, but it would probably be worth about a million pounds today.

At just after 10.30 we saw the jawless wonder staggering down the hill a bit the worse for wear towards Marvin's front gate. Dad ushered me towards the park entrance and said to me, 'When I give the word, let go of the dogs.' Jawless fumbled for the latch and, as he was going through the gate, Marvin flipped the switch that turned his front porch light on. The shock of seeing the wild and overgrown front garden flooded with light almost knocked Jawless off his feet. But that was nothing, because just at that moment the White Lady appeared from her hiding place behind a massive shrub. She looked resplendent with her most glisteningly white garb shining under the bright light. She hissed, then lunged at him, her long slender brilliant white fingers reaching towards him. Then she screeched and let out an almighty cackle, her African features beaming terror into his pathetic little heart. His jaw would have dropped, if he had one.

He turned and bolted out the gate as fast as he could. He dashed back up the hill and, just as he was passing the entrance to the park, Dad nudged me and said, 'Now!' I let loose the dogs, who went sprinting after him. They had been jumping up and down when I had the leads held tightly in my hands, but when I let go and they saw this figure running past they went completely mad. They chased him, slobbering and gnashing at Jawless' heels in a frenzy of barking and frothy spittle. He was almost tripping over his inebriated legs as Dad and I watched the dogs in hot pursuit.

He was panting by the time he'd got a hundred yards further up the hill when the third prong of the White Lady's master plan gloriously unveiled itself. Twinkly-lights bicycle-helmeted man thrust his head menacingly out from behind a parked van like an evil living-dead Christmas tree and loosed his much fiercer dog to join the pack. It was an incredible sight to see, and such an ungodly racket of dogs barking had seized our normally quiet, leafy little hill. Jawless was yelping in terror and it literally made my year when he stole a glance behind him. There was real fear in his big round blood-shot eyes as he jolted his head forward again (his lower lip playing catch up a second later).

He was starting to slow down by the time he reached the top of the hill but he must have thought he was in hell when suddenly the bush he was standing next to rustled and the crazy old woman joined in the fray. She let out such an unholy scream of infernal gibberish that Jawless must have leaped three feet into the air. He ran full tilt down the other side of the hill with the gnashing canine teeth of the three dogs still after him.

Making a row in public! Playing with wild animals! For a kid with conservative African parents this just never happened. I was whooping my head off at the bottom of the hill when Dad cuffed me hard on the back of the head. 'Shut up, bastard! What would your mother say? Stop shouting!' I looked up at Dad, rubbing my head where he'd boxed me and he said, 'A tiger does not need to proclaim its tigritude.'

The White Lady had joined us by now and soon bicycle-helmet man and the bush woman were standing next to us too. We were all laughing together when Marvin emerged from his house with a Thermos of tea. He couldn't stop thanking us each in turn as we stood drinking from a handful of billycans he'd brought out with him.

The Bush Woman brought out a little bottle of whisky and poured a shot in for herself, Dad, Marvin, the White Lady and Helmet Man, but when I pushed my cup up towards her I got nothing but a fiery look. The dogs were beginning to circle back down the hill as Dad and I made our way home to Mum who, when she heard the story, said we were totally mad and should be locked up. We were still giggling a bit as Dad tried to describe what the fleeing man looked like by pulling a face that simultaneously mimicked total terror and a lack of jaw. I can tell you that you need both hands to pull that kind of face.

10

WHEN I WAS ABOUT fourteen, Mum and Dad moved again into a big house in Balham. They still live there. Green house, red door if you're passing by. But when we moved in we only took the top floor, so it still meant only three bedrooms. To make matters worse, since coming back to England, Mum had started having kids again. We now had a new sister: Andrea. So it was Albert, Chris and I in one room and Stella, Cordelia and the newborn Andrea in the other. It was much worse for the girls because they had to help out with the youngest and a newborn baby is a pretty rubbish roommate. These days, lots of my friends have kids and some of them let the baby stay with them in their bedroom for months or even years on end. Not so in my family. A month in the marital bed and then into a crib next door they go. That doesn't mean that the baby stops crying half the night and I'd often see Stella going to school exhausted after a rough experience of screaming baby and frequent fly-by-night feeding visits from Mum.

When we first moved into that house, we shared it with a nasty old couple who lived downstairs. Mum and Dad used to say to us, 'Go on. Jump up and down!' and, sure enough, a year or two later this poor harassed couple moved out and we bought the whole place. But to start with it was just as usual. Not enough bedrooms; too many children. The only benefit was that it had a huge garden.

Now, of course, we couldn't play in our own garden as it was jointly owned with the couple downstairs and every square foot that was allocated to us was immediately built up with sheds and huts, each of which was straight away filled with hoarded junk. Mum and Dad wouldn't let us go anywhere near them in case we damaged the precious carburettors and reclaimed kitchen units they'd carefully saved. But next door was different. The house next door to us had been derelict for years and although we never went inside the building we could climb the wall and muck about to our heart's content in their overgrown garden.

My base of operations was down the bottom of the garden around the overgrown brick foundations of what must have once been a big outhouse. On the weekends, I'd spend all afternoon doing army crawls and fending off imaginary attackers down there, with Stella looking on as if I'd lost the plot and occasionally joining in. Even though he was three years older than us, Albert also liked to hang out in the garden. He'd stay near the broken-down old house because there was a huge square concrete pit dug out from the basement down that end. It was a storey below ground level and, with its smooth straight walls going straight up ten feet on all sides, it was totally out of sight. He'd found an old table and some chairs and, due to the lack of privacy indoors, he'd hang out down there doing his homework or reading magazines. He was adamant that we were not allowed in.

I'd spend hours carefully avoiding imaginary snipers to sneak to Albert's pit where I'd throw pebbles and stones down at him. When he snarled back at me and stomped around, I'd shout down at him, 'Ay! Ay! Anansi the spider is on the loose,' because even at the age of seventeen he already had very hairy legs. Only when it rained would he let me down to join him. I'd climb down the precarious sheer wall of his concrete pit using a tower of flimsy wooden boxes that Albert had stacked up to help him get in and out. Deadly enemies until bad weather struck, Albert and I would shelter from the rain under a huge tarpaulin and I'd tell him my plans of how I'd defend the garden should an intruder try and take over (as if they'd have the balls!).

Then one day an intruder did turn up to ruin my make-believe games. The house was suddenly bought by someone who started to do it up. A lot of builders were in and out, and a lot of gardeners came around too. We thought it would be a rich white family that would move in, but to our surprise it was a single black woman who could be seen coming in and out of the house at odd hours. She was always dressed in elegant clothes and I started peeping at her to try and figure out what she was up to.

To make matters even more interesting, she began to be seen outside in her garden dressed in a leotard doing odd sorts of weird exercises. She seemed to spend hours stretching and then she'd make odd poses and hold them for minutes at a time. As she was dressed in her skintight leotard, Albert was also extremely interested in what she was doing but together we couldn't figure it out.

And then one day we saw a van pull up outside and two men offload a piano into the house. She was out there with them, fretting and browbeating the men as they moved the huge instrument indoors. This was the late eighties and it was fun to see a single black woman out in the street talking down to white men. We thought maybe she was a queen or something because her demeanour was so regal.

After the piano was loaded in, we started to hear her singing.

Except she didn't seem to be singing songs that we recognized. She just sang notes going up and down and up and down, again and again. Mum used to complain a lot, saying, 'What is that racket? Is she killing a cat over there? Who is this bush woman with no husband?'

One Sunday, we were all at home, tearing down the house with our usual screams and caterwauling, when she came round to our house and banged on the front door. We thought she was coming to complain, but instead she came in and introduced herself to us. She was dressed in the kind of trouser suit that you would normally see on a man and she had a bag of sweets with her. All of us kids immediately stopped what we were doing and crowded around her – except for Albert who cowered shyly in the corner.

She said that she was called Fola and had just moved to London from Paris. When she revealed her Nigerian name, Mum immediately warmed to her and began to speak to her in Yoruba. 'How now, sista! *Ekaro* (good morning).'

Fola was a little taken aback. 'Oh sorry, dear. I don't speak the language.'

'Neither can we,' piped up Stella.

'Speak when you are spoken to! This is Stella, Stephen, Chris, Cordelia, Albert, Andrea and the baby is sleeping. Albert! What are you doing over there? Tuck in your shirt! And stop holding that book in front of you! Come and say hello!' Mum always said that she gave us English-sounding names because she wanted us to speak English and she was confused that this Fola, who had a Nigerian name, couldn't speak Yoruba. I always thought her decision to call me Stephen really had nothing to do with what language she wanted me to speak. I was born at St Stephen's Hospital in Chelsea so you can tell how hard she had to look around before deciding on my name. Not a lot of imagination.

My twin sister should count herself lucky she wasn't named 'Hospital'.

'Not at all, sorry. I was born here.' Mum couldn't understand this.

Fola revealed that she was in London to work on a West End show called *Cats*. I was strangely intrigued by this, but my mum brushed it aside and was more interested in her personal life. 'So do you have a husband?' It turned out she was married to a Frenchman who was still in Paris, but who would be arriving soon to live next door as well. Mum was shocked that Fola was married to a white man. 'Oh well, my dear. At least you are married.'

She then explained that she would sometimes be heard practising scales next door with her piano and if it was too loud or disturbing to us then we should come round and tell her so. Now this really wrong-footed Mum who had spent the better part of seventeen years apologizing for her noisy brood. Fola then dished out sweets to all of us and Mum looked on disapprovingly. She had made firm friends with the kids, but Mum had taken an instant dislike to her.

And so the mystery of Fola was solved and we tried not to get in each other's way. She would practise her singing and her dance moves in the daytime when we were at school and by the time we were screaming and shouting in the evenings she would be out at work. I was impressed by this elegant black woman who would come home late at night and step out of a black taxicab and into her home as if it was nothing. Although I'd lived in London all my life I'd never been in a taxicab.

On Saturdays, when we were at home we'd watch from the upstairs window as she practised and exercised in the garden and we'd push our ears against the wall as she sang her scales. Sometimes she'd sing, 'La, la, la, la,' and sometimes it was more like she was spitting: 'Cha, cha, cha, cha.' It sounded a bit like she was kissing her teeth the way that Mum and Dad sometimes did when they were annoyed. But in a tuneful way. We weren't allowed to kiss our teeth at home and Mum would shout at us if we did. 'Hey! Get to your room! Brush your teeth! Don't kiss them!'

After a few weeks of watching her from our upstairs window, she clocked us and gestured for us to come down and join her. We well knew how to climb over into her garden by now and so me, my sister and Albert easily scaled the wall and sat with her cross-legged on the grass.

'What are you doing?' asked Stella, who was never embarrassed to ask whatever questions came into her head.

'I'm practising being a cat,' Fola replied. 'It's not easy, you know. You have to be able to think like a cat to be able to move like a cat.'

'How do you do that?' asked Stella.

'First, you start with the face. You have to twitch your nose like this.' And she twitched her nose. 'Then you have to be able to preen yourself.' And she started to rub her cheek against her shoulder. We all copied her. 'Ah! You're very good at it. I should have known you were such good cats since you are able to climb over the wall so easily. Maybe you have done it before?' She looked at us and Albert and I squirmed guiltily. 'Don't look like that. A cat should be able to go where she pleases. A cat never asks for permission. She just does and everywhere she goes she is at home.' Stella smiled at this one. 'Watch kittens. It's all about attitude!' And with that she rolled over and sprang up onto all fours but staying very close to the ground. Then she reached far ahead of herself with one arm and then reached far ahead with the other and slinked slowly along the ground extending each of her legs to the fullest before pulling them in tight to catch up with her body.

She really looked like she was lost in her own world as she prowled around all of us. Then suddenly she sprang ahead and clasped her hands together an inch in front of her face as if catching prey. 'I caught it!' She shouted out triumphantly before making as if to eat whatever she had between her paws and licking her lips.

That night we maddened Mum and simply confused Dad by pretending we were cats at the dinner table, meowing and catching the food in our hands before gobbling it down until Mum said, 'Ah! What are you doing! If you want to behave like an animal you can go and live outside in the garden. If I sent you back to Nigeria what would they say?'

'They would say you have monkeys for children and you didn't give them a pair of shoes until they were thirteen years old!' said Dad.

'Ah! Who bore monkeys?!'

'Dad. Can we go and see *Cats*? Fola says she can get us tickets to the show whenever we want. We could get a taxi home with her afterwards.'

'You leave that woman alone. She must have put a spell on you.' I was not deterred and I still made a habit of saying hello and goodbye to Fola whenever I saw her, until one day she even invited me into her home. When I went in, I saw that it looked nothing like ours. Where we had bin bags full of old newspapers she had nice wooden furniture and paintings. All over the walls there were photographs of Fola and her hands were always covered in jewels in the pictures.

'Let's go to the kitchen and we'll have some tea,' she said. I was under strict instructions from Mum and Dad never to accept food from her in case she had put something in it to bewitch me. I could never be 100 per cent sure when they were joking, but tea seemed safe enough, so I followed her in.

I went into her kitchen and there was a big wooden sculpture on the gas hob. 'Apparently that is for cooking,' said Fola, gesturing towards the cooker. It was spotlessly clean like it had never been used. She put the kettle on and told me to get some milk from the fridge. I didn't have to worry about accepting any food from her as there was no food at all in the fridge. There was just a carton of milk and a lot of funny-shaped wine bottles that said 'Moët' on the front. I asked about them and she said they were a kind of French wine that she had bought because her husband was going to come and stay with her soon.

We sat together for a long time and she told me about what it was like to work in a theatre. It sounded like a big confusing mess, with all the different people she described coming and going backstage to make the show perfect for the audience. She told me about the huge wardrobes full of clothes and the props and the orchestra pit. She told me about being nervous in the wings and about how it felt when the light hit you on stage. She said that when you were acting you forgot your nerves and you forgot who you really were. The way she described it made the whole thing sound a lot like magic and I thought that Mum might have been right about Fola bewitching people. It sounded like she did it every night for a job.

When I asked her about her husband she said that they'd met in Paris and she told me all about France. She'd studied there for a long time she told me, with a famous Frenchman who taught her how to be a clown. I thought she was joking and I laughed at this, but she looked at me like I was the biggest idiot she'd ever met. Fola said that after you have mastered the art of being a great clown then everything else is easy. And then she pulled a funny face and told me to get home before my mum missed me.

Not long after that her husband arrived from France and he was one of the most weird looking people I'd ever seen. He was the tallest, skinniest person and he had a huge ridiculous moustache. Set against her voluptuous figure, the two of them couldn't have looked more different. But there was something in the way that he moved that was just as graceful as his wife. When he walked down the street, he looked like he was constantly about to fall over or trip up but just at the last minute his body would right itself and start falling in another direction.

I bumped into them at the shop one day and Fola introduced me. This guy was also very flamboyant and after we met he insisted that I come and see the show. Later that night he came around to the house with a ticket for the following Saturday. I explained that Mum wasn't keen on my going but he was so charming that he managed to win her around. Either that or she was just anxious to get this broomstick creature off the front step and would have agreed to anything.

So on Saturday I took the bus into the West End. I got there hours early and spent the evening wandering around Charing Cross Road and Shaftesbury Avenue staring up at the huge gilt theatres. I found the show hilarious, with all of these grown men and women running around the stage in costumes so ridiculous that I could barely recognize Fola. She invited me backstage afterwards and I watched in awe as the actors stripped off their costumes and ran around half naked, laughing, drinking and hugging each other.

I received so many random kisses from the cast that by the time I left I was on cloud nine. When the bus driver looked at me like I was a madman I figured it was the goofy smile on my face, but when I got home Mum screamed, 'Look at your face! Are you a clown now?' I checked in the mirror and my cheek was covered in different-coloured make-up and I really did look like I'd escaped from the circus.

Fola was the first black performer that I had ever met up until that point. Until then I just hadn't considered the stage as a decent place for a black person to be seen. Years later, when I decided to go into comedy, my parents asked me in distress (once again), 'What do you want to waste your life for? Are you a clown?' I remembered what Fola had said back in her kitchen with a cooker that had never been used and a fridge full of champagne and thought that if it was good enough for her then it would be good enough for me.

11

IT'S FUNNY HOW OFTEN seemingly innocent things can develop a mind of their own and just run away from you completely. You can tell just one little white lie and before you know it you're on *The Jeremy Kyle Show* hooked up to a lie-detector test. I'm intrigued by that show, but the only way it could be improved is if you got rid of the lie-detector test and just hooked the guests up directly to the mains. They say that the body gives away subtle signals when you lie. Like if the person you're speaking to is staring at you without blinking, keeping their hands and legs unusually rigid then he's probably lying to you. Or he's about to have a seizure.

But everyone's guilty of the odd little white lie. I don't mind telling a lie to spare someone's feelings. Especially if the person whose feelings I'm sparing are my own. Is honesty really the best policy? When you say to someone, 'Hi, how are you?' what you want them to ay is, 'Fine thanks', not talk your ear off for half an hour about their bad knee and swollen eye.

The habit of telling lies starts as a child. Mum used to sing me that famous nursery rhyme 'Hush, little baby, don't say a word, Mama's going to buy you a mockingbird. And if that mocking bird don't sing, Mama's gonna buy you a diamond ring. And if that diamond ring turns brass, Mama's going to buy you a looking glass' and it goes on and on. How sweet, you might think, but I can tell you that was the most disappointing birthday ever.

If you have a younger brother or sister I can tell you that you will probably lie to them just for fun. For instance, my brother Albert used to always tell me that the people on TV could see you as well. I could never watch *Baywatch* again after that. He also told me that the tooth fairy gave you more money if it was somebody else's teeth. Well, I believed him and to this day my sister Cordelia still can't speak to me. Well, she couldn't speak to anybody then. Not without dribbling.

But the problem is kids don't know how to tell plausible lies. I used to write little sick notes to the teacher to get out of sports lessons and sign them from my mum. The power of the note at school was like having a get out of jail free card in your back pocket. The only problem was I just knew the names of a lot of the diseases from old books and TV, but I didn't know what they actually were. So I started with 'Stephen's got the flu', which seemed pretty safe. But after a while I had to choose another illness: diarrhoea worked well because nobody really wants to dwell on that. The teachers were suspicious when I got over appendicitis in an afternoon. When I said that I had Bell's palsy so I couldn't play rugby they knew something was up.

I wasn't the only one in school who got caught out telling stupid lies. I had a classmate who told all of us that his dad had the car KITT from *Knight Rider*. All day long he was Mr Popular until it came to the end of the day when everyone asked him where KITT was. Suddenly, the lie came crashing down around him. He actually went to the gate and talked into his lapel 'Uh, school's over now. You can come and get me.' He's in a home now.

Lies are everywhere. Annie Lennox sang 'Would I lie to you? Would I lie to you honey?' She also said, 'Of course not, Dave Stewart, I have no intention of going solo. We'll be together for ever.' In fact, lies are so prevalent that most of us can just translate them to truth in our heads. 'I lost your email' means 'communicating with you is not important to me'. 'At least I've got my health' means 'my life has been a total failure'. 'I can't believe we reached our thirtieth wedding anniversary' means 'I can't believe I haven't killed you yet'. 'A for effort' means 'you talentless loser'. And 'Can you keep a secret?' means 'I expect you to post this on Facebook within the next ten minutes'.

When you start afresh in your life, for example if you get a new job, move to a new city or change schools or colleges, you can reinvent yourself. In other words you can tell bold-faced lies about who you are and where you come from. I had to move schools very frequently as a kid and the main effect on me of moving so much was that I constantly had to make new friends repeatedly. Some of the schools I was in for such a short amount of time that I could literally have told them anything and been out of there before anyone had time to fact-check. The problem was that the frequent moves always came out of the blue. So I never knew if my new school was the kind where I could get away with the 'I am the Prince of Nigeria' type of big lie or if it was more of the 'of course I have a girlfriend but she lives in Whitstable and doesn't have a phone in her village' kind of little lie situation.

On one occasion I got badly caught out with a fib. What began as a little white lie grew into a monster whopper and it cost me a lot to get out of it. It was when I was sixteen and I had just started at sixth-form college. I told all of my new classmates that I was related to 5 Star. I told them that Denise, Stedman, Doris, Lorraine and Delroy were all my first cousins. Looking at those names I thank

God that it's not the eighties any more. Who would call their child Doris these days and expect them to reach super stardom? Names in show business are important. With a name like Whitney Houston a star is born. Gene Pitney ditto. But what if they were to get married? Whitney Pitney would never have worked on stage.

Naturally, with 5 Star appearing on *Top of the Pops* all of the time, my friends were huge fans and they all asked if we could get tickets to see them when they came to town. I said, 'Yeah sure,' hoping that everyone would forget about it or I'd have to move again before I'd have my hand forced. Unbelievably only a couple of weeks later someone came into college saying 5 Star would be playing at the Wimbledon Theatre and that it would be the perfect time to go and see them. I was seriously in the shit. Sixteen years old, at a new college and trying to make friends. There was the potential here for a kind of social catastrophe that would have meant changing my name to Whitney Pitney and moving to Brazil.

I decided that there was nothing for it but to try and style it out. I actually went to Ticketmaster and bought five tickets for the concert, marched proudly into school and gave them to my friends. My entire life savings to date gone in one fell swoop. But then what's a sixteen-year-old going to do with money if he hasn't got any friends to hang out with? What made it worse was that this was the very first concert I'd ever been to. So not only had I been forced to spend a fortune on tickets for my new 'friends', but I wouldn't even be able to relax and enjoy the concert because I'd be so busy having to keep up the pretence. 5 Star really were my favourite band and I'd have loved to go with Stella. But that wouldn't have worked because she is incapable of lying and would have just laughed in my face if she found out the predicament I was now in, and told everyone what an idiot I was being.

So the magical night came around and we were all at the front of the theatre dancing away and everyone was having a great laugh. Except for me who had to spend the whole time making eye contact and waving at the singers. After a while they even acknowledged me. Not by waving back or smiling at me but more by making eye contact with their security and motioning in my direction. I stopped waving for a bit at that point.

After the show finished, my friends were all trying to get me to take them backstage to meet the band. I even approached the roped-off entrance to the VIP area, but as the security guard saw me approach he physically turned me around and pushed me away. I had to go back to my friends and tell them that there wasn't a backstage area at all and that the band had gone home. I just hoped that they'd failed to notice the raucous music emanating from behind the door and a steady stream of sexy young hipsters funnelling in behind us to party the rest of the night away.

So I'd managed to get away with it and if anyone guessed that I was bullshitting they never said anything to me about it. I stayed friends with those guys until I finished my A levels, so it was £75 well spent. However, from then on I learned to keep my mouth shut.

That wasn't the first time that I'd claimed a famous person was my relation. It always seemed like a good way to get attention and I even tried it at primary school. This was less to make friends and more to stop the kids from making fun of me and pushing me around. Being the only black kid (except for my sister) gave me a certain notoriety.

The James Bond film *Moonraker* had just come out at the cinemas and everyone was raving about it. Although we were all too young to get into the cinema, everyone had bootlegged copies of the film since most of the other kids' parents were market traders (or in prison). I didn't get what the fuss about Roger Moore was all about – he was nothing compared to Sean Connery – but I always thought the character Jaws was really cool with his big smiley face full silver teeth and his ability to eat metal. In fact for years I thought the Steven Spielberg film *Jaws* was going to be a feature-length movie about the big friendly giant who wanted to eat Roger Moore, and was disappointed at Christmas time when I tuned the TV in to catch *Jaws* only to be confronted by a long movie about a big fish.

One day in the playground I told a pretty bold-faced lie that would go on to haunt me. Yes, you guessed it. I used to say my mum was Shirley Bassey. Kids, as I've mentioned, will believe almost anything, and they believed me. For once everyone gave me loads of attention and not as a prelude to chasing after me and trying to hang me up by my coat again. And I milked it like any kid would. I talked about how she'd got to meet James Bond in the flesh and how next time she'd promised to take me with her on location. I was going to drive the James Bond car with her. I was going to go to America with her. I was going to meet Q, M and all the rest of them.

The story went around the school like wildfire and for the rest of the week I was a mini superstar. It was amazing and even the teachers got wind of it. On Friday the head teacher came up to me tentatively and asked me if my mum was really Shirley Bassey. I said, 'Yeah she is you know! Shirley Bassey, that's just her stage name. Lots of singers use them.' Well, she was no genius herself, being a primary school teacher at a school that the local education authority classed as just one rung above a young offenders institute. She bought it and she asked me if I could get my mum, Shirley Bassey, to come and open the school fête. A teacher who would normally just ignore me in the playground or shout at me in class was actually treating me with respect. I have to admit that I got a bit caught up in the moment and I said yes, of course she would come.

It wasn't until several hours later when I was home that I had time to think about what I had said. I was only eight years old but already I hated school. Mum and Dad knew that I was being bullied by the other kids and it was going to get a lot worse if the school fête came around and there was no one to open it. I'd have to get her to come one way or another. That night at dinner I went for it.

'Mum, there's something happening at school.'

'Is it those white children again? What have they done to you this time, my boy?'

'No, it's nothing like that. They're having a school fête next week. And they always get one of the mothers to come and open it. This year they want you to do it.'

'This year? Why have I never been asked before?'

There was no point in mentioning Shirley Bassey or James Bond as Mum would have no idea who either of them were. She did, however, like the idea of being invited to the school fête. Mum and Dad never went to any school events. From parents' evenings to school plays, the Amos household were mysteriously left off the mailing list. So Mum actually jumped at the chance and agreed.

I basked in everyone's attention for the next week and quickly the big day arrived. It was the typical cheap school fête held under a tarpaulin cover in the rainy car park. There was a stale cake sale and a raffle and a little display of the kids' finger painting and that was about it. Normally, I wouldn't even have wanted to go, but this time I couldn't wait. It was a Saturday morning and Mum dressed up for the occasion. She arrived at the school gates in Dad's car and when she stepped out of the car all the kids surrounded her in awe. Mum has a way of oozing class when the occasion fits, but with all the adoration she was receiving she didn't let it get to her head. She knew that these were the kids who were bullying my sister and me and she made sure to say a few choice words to them.

'Ah. You mouse-faced child. How sweet. Are you a boy or a girl? It is hard to tell with those clothes on.'

'Ah, little boy. Tell me do you wash your hair every week or every month? Your mother should buy shampoo.'

'Hello, little girl. You shouldn't chew chewing gum. It makes your cheeks fat. Oh! You aren't chewing chewing gum? Don't worry about it, little chipmunk cheeks.'

'Are you looking for something on the grass or do you always have a hunchback?'

Mum was having a ball and when one of the kids (Hunchback) came up to her and asked if she could sing the James Bond song, she said 'Sure, why not? Yes, my dear. I will sing you the James Bond song.' And then to the tune of 'Camptown Races' she sang, 'James Bond, James Bond, James Bond Bond! James Bond! James Bond! James Bond Bond Bond, James Bond Bond! James Bond Bond Bond Bond!'

The kids loved it! The teachers loved it! (They really weren't that smart at my school.) I couldn't believe that everyone bought it and really thought that Mum was Shirley Bassey. You have to remember that this was back in the early eighties and the teachers were always getting my sister and me confused. When we pointed out that we were not only different people but different sexes, they just said, 'Well, all black people look the same. Don't they?' Well, guess what? To them all black people really did look the same because they asked Mum to come back and open the fête two years running.

Mum really stood up for me that day at school. After that fête, the worst of the bullies diverted their attention to pulling the wings off flies. It's a shame that neither your mum, your dad nor the sick notes that they used to write to get you out of shit can follow you throughout the rest of your life. Otherwise, the next time I have to perform at a rowdy late-night gig in Leeds and the compere says, 'Amos! Get up on that stage and make the crowd laugh.' I'll just be like 'No. I got a note from my mum. She says no way. Not in these shoes. They're brand new from the shop.'

12

LOVE IS ONE OF those elusive things that everyone is constantly on the lookout for. Pubs and bars exist to exploit the fact that we will do almost anything to find it. I mean, who hasn't walked down to their local town centre late on a Friday night and thought, Hmmm. Maybe love is in that Yates' Wine Bar. You go in, drink too much, and the next morning you wake up to find that Chewbacca is lying next to you? Or who hasn't woken up in a stranger's house, empty beer bottles strewn across the floor, Ginsters' pies smeared against the wall. You drag yourself to a stranger's bathroom mirror only to realize that YOU are Chewbacca. Just me? Oh well.

And what is love? Barry White seems to be the only person able to describe properly. Which is weird because it seems to be the number one concern of most music, art, theatre, films and everything else. It's something that we think we're going to like because everyone tells us it's so great but we have no idea what it is; it's a bit like using Twitter. There are a lot of odd sayings about love. You can be 'lovesick', 'love-struck', and Mum used to say, 'Ah! Love! You'll know it when it hits you,' which makes love sound dangerous, violent and quite sinister.

But I have been in love. It struck like lightning, spun me out on a whirlwind of intensity, and then spat me out like the dried-up husk of a blood-drained corpse by a vampiress who ruined my life and tore my heart to shreds. BITCH!

Anyway, my love story starts in a branch of an Olympus Sports shoe shop based in Tooting. I had just turned eighteen and was doing part-time work in the evenings and at weekends to make a bit of extra cash and to get me out of the house. I had always taken part-time jobs ever since I was legally allowed to because if I stayed at home I was forced to work around the house for free. The money at Olympus was not really good and Mum and Dad always took most of it anyway to help them pay for bills and food, but it was better than nothing. I remember once asking Mum to let me have the whole pay cheque and she said, 'Don't talk like that to me, I brought you into this world and I will take you out of it!' while holding up a frying pan just to make her intentions totally clear.

The best thing about the job was that Dustin or other school friends could come and hang around in the shop with me. Plus, I could get a good discount for everyone on cool trainers. I was in heaven in that shop, because my parents thought that when it came to shoes or trainers practicality always won over fashion. They thought it was a waste of money buying name brand trainers. I remember one time my mate got a fantastic new pair of Nikes and I went home and told Dad. The next day he bought me a pair of shoes from the market. They were called Abibas and they cost £3. They only had one stripe. I said, 'Dad, you can't send me to school like this. I need two more stripes.'

'You want more stripes? Then paint them on!'

And the kids had been cruel to me. They'd see my Green Flash plimsolls and come up to me in the playground singing, 'Let us

go to Tesco's, where Stephen buys his best clothes. De la la la.'
Plus Green Flash made my feet look really big. They looked like
clown shoes on me. To be honest, I do have totally massive feet
and was sporting size thirteen shoes by the time I was twelve. I was
so embarrassed about my huge feet that for two years I wore shoes
four sizes too small and later on in life, guess what? I have a crooked
cock. So let that be a lesson to you.

The work was not really interesting as few people came into the
shop to actually buy anything. In that particular area of South
London most of the locals were too busy concentrating on benefit
fraud to worry about footwear. One Saturday, I was working in
the shop when, completely out of the blue, this stunning blonde
bombshell walked into the store with her parents. As they browsed
around the shop, she kept looking at me furtively over the displays.
I figured that she must like me, but with her parents in the shop
we couldn't do much more than steal glances at each other. There
was an animal magnetism at work whenever we made embarrassed
eye contact. It was that slightly creepy teenage behaviour when
you're trying to show that you like someone while resisting the
hormonal urge to run headlong into each other's arms and start
copulating wildly in front of the shoe polish section.

Her parents came up to the desk and bought her a pair of the
newest Nike Air trainers. My heart was thumping when I took the
shoe box from her. I thought I'd try to sound professional and
stylish to impress her and so I entered into the sales pitch. 'Oh.
These come with a free pair of shoe deodorizing insoles.' I realized
suddenly what I was saying. 'They just slip into the shoe every
night and stop any . . . y'know . . . bad smells . . . from . . . staying
in the shoe . . . not that you have any need for them . . . They
don't even work anyway. Just a gimmick really.' Oh please God!
Let the world open up beneath my feet and swallow me whole.

The girl went bright red and sort of laughed as her dad handed over the cash and they left. She gave me a little backward glance on her way out of the shop, though. Well, you fucked that one up, Stevie, I thought to myself.

The next day as I waited at the bus stop for school I was still daydreaming about that girl and imagining all of the impressive things that I should have said to her instead of offering her a cut-price remedy to smelly feet. I was so busy daydreaming that I barely noticed the really fit girl wearing a hot school uniform standing and looking at the bus schedule, until I saw that she was wearing the newest Nike Air trainers. Oh shit! It was her. What do I do? I should talk to her but what to say? 'Hi there. Did I see you last night at Olympus Sports?'

'Oh my God. It's you.' She had an amazing accent. The she looked me up and down in my school uniform (replete with my Dunlop Green Flash trainers). 'You go to school? I thought you must be older.' I smiled broadly at that. It's odd that a phrase works as a brilliant compliment when you're eighteen but when you're twenty-eight it would get you a slap. The same principle works in reverse as well. Tell an eighteen-year-old boy he's cute and you won't get very far. Tell me that I'm cute now and it's different story – and you can find me on Facebook if you want to try.

'Yeah. People often say I look older. I've always been pretty mature for my age.' An awkward silence descended as I played nervously with the lunch money in my pocket. 'Those shoes are looking pretty fly.' She looked confused. 'They look really good on you, I mean. Where are you from?'

'I'm Hungarian.'

'Wow. I've never met a Hungarian before. What brings you to the Big Smoke?' Bollocks! Even I knew that was lame. 'I mean what brings you to London?'

'My dad's got a job here. I didn't want to come. Look at what they have me dressed as. I look like a little kid. In my country you don't have to wear uniforms. That's why I asked them to at least get me some *fly* shoes.' She smiled.

'Well you look great to me.' Was that pervy and weird? Probably. 'I don't like wearing school uniform either, but at least it's my final year and I'll be out of there by summer. I can't wait.' That was better. 'Yep. Out into the world on my own.'

She was warming up to this. 'Me too. My parents want me to go to university but I just want to get a job like you and move out of home.'

'Yeah. In six months' time my mum and dad won't see me for dust. I'll just be . . . blowing in the wind.' I didn't know what I was talking about.

'Wow. So you're a free spirit. Just like me.' I was really falling for this girl.

'Yeah. You can count on it. Signed, sealed and delivered.' Wait a minute. Was I really saying this?

'Yeah, me too. I just need to pass the final exams.'

'Don't you worry 'bout a thing.'

'Hold on. Are you just quoting Stevie Wonder lyrics at me?'

'No! Stevie Wonder? Who's he?' My foot tasted bitter in my mouth.

'Maybe I can play you some of his songs sometime.'

'I'd like that a lot. You could always come back to the store.'

'OK, maybe I will. I like the shoes. It's just that I don't like the laces. They're boring. Maybe I should come round to your shop again and see if you have anything that is a bit more . . . funky.' If you've never heard someone with a Hungarian accent say the word 'funky' then you should find one and get them to say it to you right now. Either that or I was delirious with desire. She could probably have said, 'I have some really funky navel fluff,' and I would have still been completely bowled over.

'Yeah. We've got loads of laces. I work there pretty much every day after school. And at weekends.'

'All right. I'm coming to see you after school today.' The bus crested the hill and sped towards us. When it arrived she got on, but I told her that I had to wait for a different bus, which was a lie but I didn't want to screw it all up by continuing my weird and awkward conversation. She'd said she might come round to see me! That was enough of a result for me to actually float to school. Plus, considering the state I was in and the nonsense I was talking, another ten minutes in her company might have seen the potential for a date in the future be replaced with the potential for a restraining order.

All day at school I just wasn't myself. I had all of these strange new feelings. How do you know if you're in love? You can't concentrate. Your palms are sweaty. Butterflies in the stomach. You can't eat. Is that love? Or is that malaria? Well, whatever it was, I had it bad.

After school, I ran to the shop and for the next four hours my face was glued to the front door, but she didn't arrive. I was totally gutted. She didn't come in the next day either and by the end of the week the fantasies I'd had of our amazing first date, subsequent marriage and children were shattered. Other fantasies involving her persisted for a bit longer but I felt sure that we would never meet again.

I'd almost forgotten about her by the following week and was working as normal when the door rang and she entered. I don't want to sound bitter about it but there is a difference between the way that boys and girls flirt and date. When a guy says he'll come around and see you after school he either does what he says or he doesn't and you never see him again. Girls are different. They get you all worked up and excited to see them. Then they don't turn up and it's only after the whole thing has blown over and you're getting back to normal – *then* they turn up and throw you for six again. She sauntered up to the cashier's desk.

'Remember me?' she said suggestively.

'Of course I remember you. I didn't think you were going to come.'

'Sorry. I was busy for the last few days.' Yeah, right, of course you were. Vixen who had my heartstrings twirled around your little finger. 'So what colour laces do you think I should go for?'

I looked at the laces display and just said the first colour I saw. 'How about green?' Green. The colour of bogeys and mould.

'Do you think I'd look good in green?' She looked unsure and I corrected myself.

'How about a nice pair of red laces? I'll even do them up for you.' It worked. The next thing you know I was in very close proximity to this lovely sexy girl, lacing up her shoes. Before I knew it, the conversation unfroze and we were chatting away very happily on those teeny-tiny stools that shoe shops and children's libraries seem to have the monopoly on.

She said her name was Viola Kovach. We chatted about the snooty English girls she had to go to school with and how she missed her friends back home. Talking to her, I suddenly felt very proud and grown up. I played the worldly wise man to this girl and quietly forgot that I still had a curfew at home and shared a bedroom with my younger brother Chris. I went for broke.

'So. Would you like to go out with me sometime? I could show you around the area.'

'That would be great.' She paused a moment. 'How about this weekend? Saturday after you finish working here?'

'Yes, great. I get off at five. Come around here and we'll do something fun.'

'It's a date!' The magic words at last. She offered to pay for the laces but I said they were on me and she was out the door.

I couldn't believe how easy that had been! A date for Amos! By Saturday I was psyched beyond belief. She turned up on cue at five o'clock and it was on. I changed out of my work clothes and together Viola and I stepped out onto Tooting High Street. Now I have to point out that I was only eighteen and not a very worldly eighteen-year-old at that. Not knowing any better I decided to take her out to McDonald's. A pathetic date nowadays but back in the late eighties people still thought of McDonald's as a treat. Who am I kidding? It was a rubbish choice. But there were slim pickings to choose from in those days in Tooting. It probably should have badly backfired but it just so happened that there was still no McDonald's in Hungary at the time and so Viola was actually a little bit impressed.

'A quarter pounder with cheese meal for the lady and for me. Hmm. Chicken nuggets. Six or nine nuggets?' I was completely broke but tried to style it out. 'You know, I had a really big lunch. Maybe – can I get just get three nuggets?'

Viola laughed. 'Hey! I'm from communist Hungary, remember. Back home the guy doesn't always have to buy the girl dinner. I've got this one.' And she produced a tenner. After we'd munched our way through the food, she suggested that we go and have a drink. Again, I had to plead no money and so we bought a few beers and went to sit in the park together. We got a bit tipsy and, as it began to rain, she huddled up with me under my big jacket. Just as I was about to suggest that we head home, she kissed me right there in the middle of the park.

There's something about a first kiss that is even more

memorable and amazing than the first time you have sex. I think it's because before you full-on lose your virginity you do a bunch of other things that aren't quite sex but that feel pretty close. But your first kiss is the first time you have any sexual contact with anyone and it is completely mind-blowing. I remember meeting Viola in that park pretty much every day for the rest of the week and all we did was kiss. That was sort of a relief because when you're an eighteen-year-old conversations run a bit like this:

'God, I hate school so much. It's such a drag,' I'd say.

'Yeah, me too. I'm totally going to fail all of my A levels,' Viola would reply.

'You know I haven't even picked up a book yet,' I'd say.

'I don't even own any of the books,' Viola would reply.

'Tell me about it. I don't even know *how* to read . . . Erm, wait a minute.' When I'd say something really stupid Viola would just pretend I hadn't and kiss me. It was probably the most hassle-free relationship I've ever had.

By the beginning of the spring term at school, we were hopelessly, disgustingly, in love with each other. We'd go to the cinema together and sit at the back giggling and being shushed by everyone. We'd hold hands and moon at each other. OK, it was pretty sickening, but when you're young and in love for the first time you don't have much of a frame of reference for how to behave. She said she wanted to meet my family and that she wanted me to meet hers. Obviously, it was totally out of the question for her to come to my place, but I was happy to go around and see hers.

Before I knew it, I was going around to her house for dinner often and I was on first-name terms with her mum and dad. Viola was an only child and so dinnertime at their house was a lot less hectic than at mine where you had to get in there quick or be left with an empty plate. Everyone took their time and they had conversations at the table while drinking wine and beer. Her parents were really permissive and they would make a lot of public displays of affection to one another. Actually her mum was a bit creepy when she met me at the door. She would kiss me on the cheek and give me a hug, which would linger for a bit too long. But I wasn't complaining and just figured that Europeans were flirtier than Brits. One night they even offered to let me stay round at their house over the weekend. I couldn't really believe what I was hearing. 'Where would I stay?'

'With Viola, of course.' Now this was so completely exciting that I almost spat out my soup.

I probably said, 'That would be GREAT!' a little bit too eagerly.

The next day I visited Albert to get some advice. He'd moved out of the family home, was staying in university halls in central London and had always been a rock of stability in the maelstrom of our family. Ever since those days back in Nigeria, Albert was the kind of guy who had never had any problem getting girls even though he was a student of chemistry. How could a guy who wore protector specs and a lab coat all day be such a magnet for the ladies? I didn't understand it. I asked him straight out: 'Albert. I've got a serious date. What do I do?'

'How serious, Stephen?'

'She's asked me to stay round at her place for the night! What do I tell Mum and Dad?' He punched me on the arm and gave me a huge hug of congratulations. He said that I could tell them I was staying with him over the weekend and I was virtually floored by the next thing he offered. He told me that I could borrow his car so that I could take her out for a drive on Saturday. I'd passed my driving test about a week after my seventeenth birthday, but in spite of my regular pleadings my dad had never ever let me use his clapped-out old Citroen. Albert even gave me sixty quid to spend!

When the weekend came around, I picked up Albert's car and virtually flew to Viola's house. I was drooling all night long and I can tell you that it wasn't the dodgy Hungarian goulash that they served for dinner. Viola's parents were being especially touchy-feely with each other that night and so when dinner was over we were pleased to be excused from the table and I went with their daughter up to her room.

We played music for a bit and started to play around. I can tell you I had never been so horny in my young life as I was that night. Just when things were getting very hot, we started to hear a weird sound. A kind of rhythmic beating sound, which at first I attributed to the music. Then we started to hear sounds that were definitely not on the Prince album I'd brought over that night (this was the *Purple Rain* period, before he turned into Satan's tiny sex doll with the New Power Generation). After a few minutes, it sounded like there was a full-on brass band playing next door. There's something about the thought of your girlfriend's parents screwing like Swedish pigs next door that can take the meat out of your bacon. Sadly, nothing happened that night.

It was a pretty uncomfortable breakfast with her mum and dad gliding around the kitchen like they'd been up all night experimenting with the *Kama Sutra* extended edition. It was a horrible feeling knowing that your mojo had been stolen by a couple of wrinkly oldies and so I was thankful when the object of my affection suggested that we go out for a drive. I jumped at the chance and the minute we were in the car together the atmosphere relaxed. I pushed play on the tape deck and Gary fucking Numan came on. A huge star in the late seventies, Gary Numan had had three number ones including the hit song 'Cars' and he'd introduced electronic synthesizers into the pop mainstream. He was Albert's favourite singer (how *did* he get so many girlfriends?) and the speakers pumped out: 'Here in my car, I feel safest of all. I can lock all my doors. It's the only way to live. In cars.' Lyrically, it's somewhere between what a special child and a hobo might say, if they were talking under water. Viola saved the day by producing a Stevie Wonder cassette and we sat back and relaxed to the beats of Stevie. Things were really beginning to look up.

We drove all the way to Hastings and stopped at a nice pub-hotel. Viola called home and told her parents that we were going to stay the night and asked me if I wanted to call mine. She was very impressed when I told her no, I didn't need to check in with Mum and Dad, I was my own man after all (quietly thanking Albert for covering for me). I had forty quid saved from work and with Albert's sixty it was a hundred pounds well spent as we ate together and went to bed together. It was, of course, fantastically short-lived, but as teenagers we had another go and in the end spent most of the night at it.

The next morning we got up very late and had a lovely pub lunch. It was gloriously relaxed and I had a couple of beers but Viola, who was on cloud nine, must have drunk most of a bottle of wine. We decided to head home and got back in the car. Stevie Wonder was blaring out of the speakers with the windows down, as we headed back up the motorway, stealing glances and letting our hands play over each other's whenever I changed gear. After about half an hour, Viola began to look uncomfortable in her seat. I closed the window and asked her if she was cold. She said she was fine, but soon began shuffling around. I asked her what was wrong and she said that she'd maybe had too much to drink and she was desperate for the loo.

We've all been there and so I did the honourable thing. I said that I'd try to pull over so that she could take a wee. She was embarrassed, but obviously extremely relieved when I pulled off onto a slip road. She gratefully got out of the car, thanking me profusely and made her way over to the verge. The grass verge had a sheer drop behind her and was very breezy, so I offered to shield her from the wind and the passing traffic, but she said no and that she was quite all right to go it alone.

It was quite precarious because she had to balance her body in a crouched position with her whole centre of gravity concentrated in one place. I too know that feeling because years later I travelled to India, a country which invented that devil's contraption called a squat toilet. I was using one of these squat toilets on a bumpy train and let me tell you I almost fell into the hole. But at the time I knew nothing of these things.

She asked me not to look, but it was hard not to as she squatted at the top of the verge. I will never forget the look of pure bliss on her face as she began to wee. Because it was the last thing I saw before her legs went flying up from underneath her as she tumbled backwards down the grass verge. Although I was madly in love with Viola it was still the funniest sight I had ever seen. She looked like a urinary Catherine wheel as she fell head under heels down what must have been an eight-foot embankment. I went running as fast as I could to the verge to make sure she was all right and there she was at the bottom in a heap. I couldn't keep the tears of laughter back as she slowly crawled up the bank. I helped her up the last few feet and she looked a right state. She had twigs and leaves in her hair like a wild bush woman and her face was smeared with mud.

She sat in silence for the rest of the journey home, looking more and more dejected. The more I tried to control my laughter, the worse my giggles got and before long she had started to cry with embarrassment. I felt terrible for her, but her tears only made the whole thing seem funnier to me. By the time we got back to South London she'd stopped crying, but when I pulled into her street and stopped the car she ran inside without saying another word to me. I called her later and asked her if she'd come and meet me in the park, but she said I was an insensitive bastard and that she never wanted to see me again.

That night I went over to Albert's flat to return his car and he asked me how it had gone. I told him that it was all over between me and Viola. I told him about the urinary Catherine wheel and he laughed his head off with me about it, which cheered me up. He told me, 'You need to find a girl with a good sense of humour. If you can't be yourself you'll never find the one. Stephen, let me give you some advice: love is like a lost fart. If you have to force it; it's probably shit.'

I'd lost my virginity and broken up with the love of my life in less than forty-eight hours but still, I thought to myself, it had been a pretty good weekend all told. I've never had another like it. To this day, I think that Viola overreacted. I thought she was being really harsh on me as, after all, I'd run to help her up. I couldn't help it if I found the whole thing amusing. Anyone would. I called her one more time that week, but she said that I shouldn't call her house any more. She swore me to secrecy over the whole urinary Catherine wheel incident, but then while we were having sex that night in Hastings she'd sworn that we'd be together for ever. So, Viola Kovach of Tooting High Street, here's to you.

13

A TAXI DRIVER ASKED me the other day, 'Here. If your parents are Nigerian and you grew up in South London, how comes you talk so posh then?'

I just said, 'Call me Miss Daisy and drive on!'

Another one of these national treasures said to me, 'What did you do before you did comedy then?'

I said, 'I studied law.'

'Do you think you'd ever go back to it?'

'Why would I?'

'Because then you could help your people. A lot of the young black men get in trouble with the law.'

'Lots of young black men like comedy as well,' I replied

But it does make you wonder about how differently things can turn out. When I was finishing school, I really did want to be a lawyer more than anything else, and how do I know if I wouldn't have been happier doing that? Sometimes I think it would be cool if there was some way to see how your life could have turned out if you'd just made a couple of decisions differently. Well, now you can: there's a computer game that people are playing online at the moment called 'Second Life' and I met this woman that said you could live a whole new life in-game these days. She said that you can choose what you look like, what job you do, buy a house anywhere in the world, have pets, fight – you can even go dancing in clubs. I read about a couple who got married on 'Second Life' and divorced without ever actually meeting. To me this seems like a world gone mad. I wonder if they ever electronically hooked up? It sounds risky to me. I wouldn't want to trust my bits to any kind of sexual computer plug-in because what if it developed a fault? For instance, I've got a printer attached to my computer at home and paper is always getting jammed inside. When that happens I either have to yank the paper out with surprising force or call in a computer repairman. I don't fancy doing that with my tool stuck in the spool.

Games have moved on since I was a kid but I've always loved them for the escapism they provide. I was around a bit before Nintendo and the Mega Drive, but what I did have was my Atari 2600 battery-powered breeze-block gaming system. It was loaded with three games and had a joystick as big as a baby's forearm. It didn't have good graphics; it wasn't in colour; and each set of massive square batteries only lasted about half an hour. In fact, my sister's Spirograph was probably more technologically advanced. I'd got it for my sixteenth birthday and my favourite game was 'Space War!' and I was still hooked two years later. No, I'm not a slow learner! I'm sure games were more difficult back then. I tried playing my nephew's PlayStation 3 game 'Little Big Planet' last year where you play a little ball of wool jumping about the place. Where's the jeopardy? Where are the spaceships? I ask you!

In 'Space War!' You played a giant flying dinosaur, who went about swallowing spaceships. It was excellent and came second place only to 'Donkey Kong', which was loaded onto the family computer upstairs. Naturally, we weren't allowed to use the family computer unless it was for educational purposes: homework only. I played it all the time though. The secret was not to get caught out – although I was often sprung by Mum.

'What are you doing?' she would bellow. I would jump.

. . ..

'Is it a toy?' Silence.

. . ..

'Who allowed you to switch it on?' I was trying to think of a good answer.

. . ..

'Hmmm?' I was paralysed with fear.

. . ..

'Am I talking to myself like a mad person?'

. . ..

'You, Mr stuff and nonsense, you want to break it?'

. . ..

Come to think of it, I wonder why Dad had even loaded a game onto the main computer at all? It was like he just wanted to taunt us with something in the house that was designed for fun but that we couldn't use. Well, that was my dad for you. This was the same man who kept the biscuits in a locked cupboard in the kitchen and if we begged him for a Rich Tea he'd maybe let us have one while shouting, 'Just take one! There are twelve in there and I'll know if you have more!'

I remember playing 'Space War!' during the summer just after I had finished my final A levels. I was in that weird time between your first life of education, school uniforms and sports days and the second life you'd have as a young man somewhere in the murky future. The coming A-level grades would decide what kind of life that would be. Maybe university, maybe that job at McDonald's where I'd be set up for life with a possible management training course leading to those five stars on my lapel? The future seemed full of possibilities.

Nobody knew what was going to happen and it was really pissing off my mum. Normally in the summer holidays, I'd have been off trying to get a job at the insistence of my parents. But this time around was different. There was no good pestering me to get my part-time job at Olympus Sports back if a full-time job at the council was what was needed. Likewise, why waste time applying for full-time positions if university was a possibility? All we could do was wait and see if I'd got the magical As or the dreaded Us. For maybe the first time in my teenage years, Mum couldn't tell me what to do, so playing computer games seemed like the perfect distraction. Plus I knew it really got under her skin. So I loved it even more.

I remember one morning I was happily playing away on my Atari when I was defeated by the lack of power, and not in the superhero sense. My hand-held gaming device screen began flickering, making it increasingly difficult to eat the spaceships and take me on to the next level. A level I was desperate to achieve. I sighed: a noise I knew so well and that I had been making repeatedly since completing my final exam. It's the noise you make when you are resigned to the fact that there is nothing more you can do.

Lost in my own imagination, a little computer-gaming scene was played out. There was I, dressed in a gleaming white, pristine starched lab coat, safety goggles on my forehead, with a serious look upon my face. I purposely entered a futuristic science laboratory, clipboard in hand, pen protruding from between my clenched teeth. Sprawled on the operating table in my imaginary lab, was an exact replica of the massive creature I had used to devastatingly devour all the spaceships in my favourite game. A full-size spaceship-eating dinosaur lolled over the table, but I had no sense of fear. As I approached the desk, the creature looked up at me with despair in its huge reptilian eyes. I instinctively shook my head.

'Nooooooo,' it cried. Actually, it was more of a Kenneth Williams' wail, which took me back. That was definitely not the sound I imagined this creature would ever make. A single tear fell down its . . . face, I guess. With hand outstretched, I rested my palm on his shoulder.

'I'm sorry, there's nothing more we can do.' We both lowered our heads. Game over. Who says computer games dull the imagination?

Checking in the drawer, I saw that I'd run out of the bumper pack of batteries that Dad had bought me as a congratulations for finishing my exams. Duracell? No! Dur-a-sell me, a cheap knock-off battery pack from the market. Thanks, Dad! The famous Duracell bunny jingle played in my head, 'They go on . . . and on . . . aaaand stop working.' So I decided to push my luck, take my life into my own hands, and try to tiptoe upstairs and turn on our family computer.

This was the last house I ever lived in with my parents. It was our big place in Balham near the Tube station, next door to Fola. Having chased the old couple downstairs out, we now had the run of the whole place – it had three floors, four bedrooms and two reception rooms. Plenty of places to hide, you might think, but you'd be wrong. The house was Mum's undisputed territory. The kids were grudgingly tolerated at best so long as we didn't get in her way. Privacy was an English word that got lost in translation for my parents. 'Privacy! What is that? You want privacy? Buy your own house!'

We had one phone and it took pride of place in the hallway.

And, aged eighteen, I still couldn't even use it without being listened to disapprovingly. On the rare occasion when someone phoned me, I would have to be very quick. 'Uh, hi! I can't talk for long . . . because Dad is staring at me!' He didn't understand that if they call you then they are the ones who pay for the call. Well, he did understand that but was just generally distrustful of the kids touching anything that could potentially cost him money.

Once my sister Cordelia made the grave error of actually dialling a number (maybe to see if the phone worked) and the next day Dad installed a lock on the dial. However the Amos kids were pretty smart and those of you old enough to remember the old rotary dialling phones will recall that you could dial a number by tapping the tone dialler up and down really quickly. So if you wanted to dial a nine you'd tap it up and down nine times and then give it a second before starting in on tapping out the second digit. At the end of the month Dad got the bill and he was like 'Ay! Ay! Who's been using the phone?'

'We don't know! You installed the lock remember?' the kids would reply smugly and Dad would look at his wife with a weary eye and mutter to himself. Amos phone hackers!

When Dad was out at work, which was pretty much all the time, Mum would patrol the house like a brave lioness patrolling the Serengeti, sniffing the air and cocking her ears to make sure there was no one up to any 'nonsense' in the house, as she put it. You had to keep your ears open in case the lioness was on the prowl. The way Mum could creep, stalk and then pounce on the unsuspecting young gazelle was like something out of a David Attenborough wildlife documentary. I used to think she had padded feet because you could never hear her coming.

That was odd because even though we had carpets, the stairs did creak. And not a gentle subtle creak, no. We lived in a horrendous Hammer house of horrors and the creaking was so loud that you could hear it not only from outside, but across the road too. Why the neighbours hadn't complained to the council remains a mystery to me. Maybe there had been complaints that I didn't know about. Councillors were probably used to getting calls saying, 'That house party over there is too loud! Turn it down!' but maybe 'That house over there is too loud. Knock it down!' would just generate confusion. I used to think the house was haunted and I remember lying awake at night, terrified of the dark, with all the sounds of the house giving me nightmares. I asked if I could have a night-light.

'No. Who is paying for the electricity? When you get a job you can have a night-light.'

I couldn't fart in that house without the whole place vibrating like the inside of a guitar echo chamber. If I was returning very late from a night out I had to tiptoe backwards up the stairs so that if I was caught I'd say I was simply going to check that the front door was locked. In all my flash gear.

Now I have big feet and I'm a big man and so tiptoeing isn't even that easy a task for me, but I was feeling bold that day. I didn't think twice about the consequences. There was nobody upstairs. What's the worst that could happen? No sooner had I pushed the floppy disk in with my finger than I heard a voice. That voice. A voice I've heard call out my name in the exact same disappointed and angry tone for eighteen years. Shit! Caught red-handed. My only chance was that technology wasn't fast in those days. I had about six minutes until the game loaded.

'Stephen! What are you doing up there? . . . Well?'

I struggled to find the right words, but still nothing came out. As I slowly turned around, there she was in all her raging glory.

'I was gonna work on my CV!' Bloody hell! Where did that

come from? That's one to go in the Rolodex of swift comebacks for use at another time.

There was definitely a shift of gear. Mum's face softened.

"Your CV? Well, I don't think you'll be needing that. Not just yet at least.'

Mum came and sat next to me. Just to the side of the computer and a bit too close for comfort. I tried to angle my wiry teenage body, both to hide the screen and position myself into something resembling the sprinter's starter position (in case I had to make a quick getaway). Any minute now, the screen is going to come to life with *DISC READY*, revealing the logo of the jungle monkey game.

'What do you mean, Mum?' I asked.

'You have a letter,' she replied with a broad grin. Sure enough in her hand she had a letter. 'Here.' She passed it to me. 'Open it.'

I looked at the front of the envelope; although it was definitely addressed to me, it was already open. I took pleasure in knowing that all my personal mail was in fact delivered to my mate's house down the road. I bit my tongue, but I wanted to shout at her, 'Ha! I win in the end, sucker!'

To keep the peace, as usual, I removed the letter, making no mention of the fact that my privacy had once again been violated. Mum looked eager: clearly it must be something good.

It was from Westminster Polytechnic. I read it.

'Read it out loud, I want to hear,' Mum said. Again, I bit my tongue and did as she requested.

'"In light of your excellent interview, we are pleased to offer you a place on the criminal justice law degree upon you achieving two Cs and one D grade.'

'Hurrah, and they are what you have been predicted as well! We will have a lawyer in the family. Praise be to God for allowing my genes to come through. *Openi fu oluwa*. Praise be to God!'

'What do you mean allowing *your* genes to come through?'

'Ah! Your father! This morning when we read the letter together he said, "With a criminal law degree Stephen could have a good career at the Citizen's Advice Bureau!" Can you believe it? No, you will be a lawyer! Sometimes I think that your father's head is not correct. *Biwon shiman shine ei*. That's how he does it!'

I smiled as she hugged me. Lost in her ample bosom, I thought that this could be the start of something new, my golden ticket out of here. I didn't care if it was a degree in criminal law or animal husbandry. It meant I could move out! Go to live in a hall of residence! Be independent! Even read my own letters first!

'So, don't think about work for now. You will enter college and no job will interfere. The student grant will even cover our living expenses.' Before I could have a chance to digest those words the logo of 'Donkey Kong' finally appeared on screen. Mum turned around and scolded me. 'Ay! What are you doing wasting your life with this fantastical nonse—' But she caught herself midway through the sentence and swallowed her words. I'd never seen that happen before! I didn't even mind getting in trouble again because I wasn't going to need computer games to escape any more. My second life had already begun.

14

BOTH DUSTIN AND I got into Westminster Poly and we moved into the same halls in Camden together as well. They were a dump by normal standards, but my standards were quite low so the leaky toilets and drab, cluttered surroundings didn't bother me at all. The rooms were tiny boxes big enough for a single bed, a sink and a desk. Everyone complained about them but for me – I was just pleased to have my very own room for the first time.

The students were from all different walks of life and some of them totally baffled me. I remember there was one really posh girl called Charlotte who lived down the corridor. She'd gone to Harrow but used to always wear dashikis and had dozens of bangles on her wrist. When she saw that I was living there she went and wrapped an African headscarf over her blonde hair and tried to make friends with me.

'Hi, Stephen, I'm Charlotte. Wicked, yeah?' She offered me her fist to touch.

'Why are you wearing that on your head?'

'I got it over the summer holidays when I went to Malawi. The plight of starving African children just got to me so much that I had to do something about it. I got my parents to sponsor me to go there and build a bridge.'

'That's nice. How does a bridge help feed the children?' That got her.

'Oh, everything was organized by my school. I had to get water from a well with a bucket and everything.' I thought of Sunday and his lesson to me in *baffing* skills and smiled. 'When I got there and saw these children looking up at me, I just felt so comfortable. Like I was coming home, you know? It changed me for ever. I may never wear Western clothes again.'

And then a month later she saw the film *Che!*, started smoking Café Crèmes and wearing a stupid beret. This was a girl who would take up any cause as long as she could wear a silly hat while doing it. Actually, the last time I saw her was a few years later in Brixton when she'd decided to really piss off her parents by becoming a squatter. She was wearing huge bomber jacket, had shaved off all her hair and was sitting by a huge sound system that was belting out dub music. She was trying to pet the feral squatter kids who were biting and scratching her back. How authentic! She must have been in heaven.

For me, being a student was an expensive business. Sure we got a grant. Sure we had accommodation provided. But that beer wasn't going to buy itself. As such, most people took whatever jobs they could get or face the stigma of being left out of the rounds at the student bar. To help me get by I took a job working at a supermarket in Camden. I went in at entry level and my job was to go around the car park and collect the trolleys. This may seem like the world's most futile and boring job. Collecting trolleys just so that shoppers could pick them up and disperse them again. And it was futile and boring. The only fun part was dangerously competing with my workmates to see how many trolleys we could collect together and then drive around like a caravan of rusty listing camels across the busy car park without crashing into a car, the wall or a pedestrian.

It was while working there that I got my first promotion. They promoted me to the shop floor so that at least I wouldn't have to freeze all day outside. It wasn't the champagne-popping experience it might have been – they made me the mince man. By which I don't mean that I stood behind the counter saying, 'Oooh. I like your beef,' in the style of John Inman. No, I made the mince. I'm sure these days the supermarket holds itself to rigorous standards but back then it didn't. The way we made mince was to take the old cuts of beef, mince them up with some fat in a grinder, and for colour? Add blood. Yum! Then we'd sell the whole lot on a half-price special and hope no one turned up with salmonella the next day.

One job that I took was actually the result of a drunken challenge. Although I'm tall and quite big now, when I was younger, I was rake thin. I virtually had a concave chest and would not have got very far in a fight. So when I noticed an advert for a job in the paper to be a security guard and told my mates about it, all of my friends laughed their heads off. So I thought that I'd show them, and applied to be a security guard on the Orient Express. And I got it.

Wow! I thought. I'd get to see the world. Mix with the glitterati. Maybe meet a rich widow who'd marry me and lead me off to a life of leisure. This was in the days before the Internet, but I should have done some research beforehand. If I'd looked into it then I would have seen that the train normally travelled from Paris to Istanbul and so when I was told to report to a railway siding in Wandsworth I should have realized that I was a bit off track. I was in fact put in charge of looking after the Orient

Express trains. But when they were stationary and getting repaired in England.

It was my job to man the security booth and check the workers' badges as they came in at eleven in the evening and then to do the same thing in the morning after they'd finished work. I literally had to sit there and say, 'Good evening. Good evening. Good evening,' with my head whipping back and forth to catch a glimpse of their security badges as they rushed past me, and do the same thing six hours later. There were about a hundred workers and so I developed a serious strain in my neck doing this job. Up until then I thought you could only get RSI in your wrist.

But being unqualified for a job has never stopped me from applying. After I finished university, I worked for an entire year for the Merton Housing Repair Department and you couldn't meet a less-handy man than me. For example, about a year ago I was on a national tour and I got a flat tyre on the way to Woking. Myself, my warm-up act and the driver were all standing by the side of the road like buffoons for twenty minutes trying to figure out what to do. The tyre was definitely flat. Was there an iPhone app that could help us? What is that thing in the boot? Is it a jack? Is it a wingnut? Is it a batwing? Could we call Batman to help us? We felt like those apes in *2001: A Space Odyssey* when they find the monolith. We ended up calling the RAC.

My point is that I'm not mechanically minded and I'm not repair minded either. Which is why I'm amazed that I managed to get the job at the Council. It was up to me to go around to people's houses once they'd vacated for whatever reason (done a runner to avoid paying rent/drug dealer/child support), spruce the place up a bit and get it ready for the next tenant. I didn't do the repairs myself but would go in with a bunch of burly builder types who'd do the actual work.

Sometimes the new tenant wouldn't be very happy with the finished result. I remember one guy who called us in because he wanted a second deadlock installed on his front door. I duly went round.

'This lock'll never do. Anyone could break in,' he declared while pounding dementedly on his own front door.

'We're only allowed to pay for one lock. But if you want another one then you can install it yourself. It looks quite solid to me.'

'Solid?! Solid?! This wouldn't keep someone out for two minutes. I know that for a fact. I'm a burglar by trade.' Well, you can't really argue with that if you want to leave the block with the same number of fingers you had when you went in. We installed a new lock for the gentleman.

Sometimes, if they'd left in a hurry, you'd get a bizarre insight into how someone had lived their life while still a tenant. Some were quite clearly totally mad and clearly obsessive. I once had to clear out a one-bedroom flat that had been rented by a 'creative' madman. What this guy had done was really weird. He'd laid car tyres flat across all the floors. Then he'd laid plywood on them to raise the floor by six inches throughout (I'm sure this all makes sense when you're tripping on acid). After that he'd had to saw off the bottom six inches of all the doors so that they could open (of course). Weirder still and completely unconnected (except I'm guessing it was very strong acid) is that he'd got someone to draw around him in red marker pen while standing against the wall. In profile with a huge erection. And if there was any doubting his clear virility, he'd traced the profile of a heavily pregnant lady in green marker on top of each of his little portraits. Going into that flat we felt like we'd entered a hall of mirrors from *The Twilight Zone*.

Aside from being a really good place to work if you are nosy, the people I worked with at Merton Council were great. When I told them I was leaving, they all clubbed together and got me a leaving card with twenty quid inside. It was like a Christmas present from your gran. We all went for a drink afterwards and I was sat next to my co-worker Leslie. She was really hilarious because she was in charge of rehousing the local travelling community who'd been given a strip of land to settle on. Before we went for a visit, she'd call to give them a chance to chuck all of their dubious plants in the bin in advance. As we'd arrive at the site, all of the men would be driving away since most of the tenants were registered as single mums to get their benefits. Leslie would always joke that they should just save the weed plants and offer her some next time.

At my leaving drinks, Leslie was very friendly and then all of a sudden she got very jumpy. She turned to the table and very earnestly said, 'Something terrible's happened. I've lost a wrap of speed on the floor somewhere. If you find it, it's yours.' And then she abruptly left. I didn't know what speed was at the time, but suddenly all of my co-workers dived for the floor. About an hour later, I had to call a friend of mine to come and pick me up in his car as my ex-boss wouldn't stop hugging me and telling me how much he'd miss me. I just thought – what a nice place to work!

Drugs are bad. And drugs and work do not go together. Although maybe the one place that they might go together could be Amsterdam. Somehow the place still seems to function. I don't know how people working in coffee shops can do things like give correct change, cash up, lock up *and* make coffee.

I went to Amsterdam for a gig a few years ago and I was sitting in a coffee shop, smoking a joint, when some guy came in and offered anyone who wanted it a day's work picking magic mushrooms in a city greenhouse. About a dozen stoned gap-year dropouts stumbled after him. I thought, That's not going to be a good day for the poor kids. They're already stoned out of their brains – I use the term loosely – and after a day of back-breaking labour that multi-coloured wizard will probably pay them with a handful of spiders. They'll be running home as fast as their tentacles can carry them. You know when you catch your brain thinking something it shouldn't be? Well, at that point, laughing to myself uncontrollably I decided it would be best to leave the coffee shop, never smoke a spliff again and go back to my drug of choice: beer.

Working at the council was pretty good compared to some of the succession of dreadful jobs I had when I was younger. Ever since I was legally able to work I've always had jobs as it was the only way I could ever get any cash to spend. I once asked Mum for pocket money and she said, 'Pocket money!? Your pocket is for your hands!' Which is never a good thing to tell to a teenage boy with holes in his pockets. It amazed me that some parents just give their kids money. What is this mysterious allowance or payment for chores that I'd heard of? We did chores for nothing. So if I wanted anything at all I had to earn the money to get it.

One of the first things Dad told me about the world of work is that you have to pay your dues. Unfortunately, he never properly explained what 'dues' were. So until I was sixteen I thought your 'dues' were a 50 per cent tax that you had to pay to your parents every week. During school holidays, I'd have a paper round and come back in from work and Dad would say, 'Ah! Stephen! Pay your dues!' And I'd have to hand over twenty quid. On top of that, Mum would always open my post so she would know exactly how much I was being paid, so I couldn't even try to be sneaky with my wages. By the time I was fourteen, all of my friends were building treehouses and Scalextric sets. I was the only one building my own letter box.

At Olympus Sports, where I met Viola, I got to earn a little bit and I got to spend a couple of months out of the house. However, it was really badly paid and so, as soon as I'd earned enough to buy a few pairs of trainers, I told the manager to go fuck himself and I quit. My dad had always told me that nothing felt better than having a job. He was wrong. Nothing feels better than quitting a job and telling your boss to go fuck himself. Actually, the manager wasn't a bad guy at all.

My record for the shortest time in employment is two hours. It was another job I'd had while at university and I'd been hired to work in the kitchen at a local greasy spoon café. Even though it was my first day on the job I admit that I had been out the night before and I was really hungover. Not only that but I'd pulled the night before and there was a nice warm person in my bed at home while I was in a hot smelly kitchen, cracking eggs onto a skillet with a pounding headache. Now this was no gourmet affair but the chef acted like he was Gordon Ramsay, running around the tiny kitchen with a bandana round his head shouting, 'Service!' Which meant two builder's teas and a bacon sarnie. He was halfway through earnestly teaching me how to butter bread when I thought, Stephen! Is this really worth the £3.50 an hour? It wasn't. I quit.

The very worst job I ever had was when I was sixteen and employed as a door-to-door salesman selling tea towels. It was unbelievable. The boss would pick us all up in a van and drop us off at the bottom of a long street and pick us up at the other end. I don't think I ever sold one tea towel. I mean, think about it. I was going to peoples' homes, the one place where they are likely to have a lot of tea towels, and offering to sell them more tea towels. It's like offering to sell dough to a baker. Plus, if you picture the scene, this was the late eighties and I was a pimply black teenager ringing on strangers' doors. Let's just say that even though I must have looked like a desperate orphan boy, no one greeted me with open arms. It was more open suspicion. The boss was like a cross between a gang master and the child catcher and I was basically playing a shit version of the children's game 'knock and run', where I always got caught.

I've quit a lot of jobs in my time but there is only one job that I actually managed to get fired from. I loved animals, but as a kid I could never have any kind of pets as my Mum and Dad hated anything that lived and required feeding that couldn't eventually be expected to earn a living for them. I was still living at home at the time and, when I saw a job in the local paper for a vet's assistant, I applied for it and got it. Looking back, I'm glad that I just got fired and not prosecuted or condemned to hell. I will never get my hands dirty like that again.

The title 'vet's assistant' turned out to be a bit of an overstatement for the actual role I was given. This was a South London vet and so we were basically like an extermination and sterilization camp for dogs that couldn't cut it in the illegal-fighting clubs of Tooting any more, or for cats who'd outgrown their litter boxes. The animals would be put down humanely by the vet and it was my job to store them in the freezer until they were collected once a week and incinerated. It was a horrible job, but I was saving to buy a car at the time so I just put up with it. I never actually saved enough to buy a car until I was in my twenties but it was a goal. You'll take any job when you're young if a babe-magnet on wheels is the prize you're working towards.

My only consolation was trying to arrange the animals into peaceful poses so that when the time came for them to be picked up they weren't frozen into weird shapes. I felt a bit like a deep-freeze taxidermist. Or the doggie Damien Hirst. Looking back, I can't believe that I put up with it. Anyway, the job was going on in a business-as-usual way with a steady stream of spayings and slayings and little Samson the Cheshire cat had just gone up to kitty heaven. The little guy was nestled in the freezer ready to be picked up the next day for cremation when we got a call from the owner. Her daughter wanted to see little Samson one last time.

When you first start out in the world of work you can take the whole 'customer is always right' thing too far. Or maybe you've not had the experience of trying to defrost a dead cat to teach you how to say, 'No. You've had your cat put down. You should have thought of your daughter's feelings beforehand.' But when you're seventeen and thinking about how sad it must be for the daughter not to have seen her favourite pet before its untimely death you say, 'Sure thing. Come on in before the end of the day', and get busy with the hairdryers. After two hours, I really felt like some kind of evil serial killer or a witch doctor. And then a miracle: Samson came back to life! No, he didn't. I'm not Jesus.

Samson looked like he'd had a very bad day at the hairdresser's and the whole vet's reception smelled like dead biscuit. Sort of dry and soggy at the same time. When the woman and her daughter came on this scene, it wasn't a pretty sight and, once the child started screaming and crying, it got a lot worse. The vet came out to see what all the commotion was about and he fired me on the spot. It was a total relief to get out of there because what started out as a totally good intention had spiralled way out of hand. It was like if you were to innocently sponsor an African child only to have a teenaged Idi Amin turn up at your door proclaiming, 'Mummy! Daddy!' (well, rather that than have him attempt to eat your friends and family).

When I got home I thought Mum would not be impressed but she actually laughed at how I'd been fired over a dead cat. She decided to tell me a story about how they deal with pets in Nigeria. 'Stephen, once when I was young my brother brought home a stray dog. But he was wild and vicious and he kept soiling the floor. One day, we came home from school and found him missing. We looked everywhere and after a while Daddy said that he had gone to live on a farm. We all knew what he meant.'

I tried to lighten the mood and be funny. 'Thats sad . . . did you still get to write to your brother?' She looked at me for a moment and had absolutely no idea what I was talking about or why I was laughing my head off.

15

SEX. IT'S VERY CONFUSING. The stress, the anxiety, the peer pressure. When do I do it? Should I be having it? Am I missing out on it? Who should I be having it with? The whole topic of sexuality is basically designed to make you go bat-shit crazy. There is even a whole branch of psychology dedicated to studying sexuality – to which I say, 'Get a real job, perverts!' And some people are even addicted to sex – to which I say, 'Get a job, perverts!'

These days there's a big debate about the sexualization of our youth and some of those points may be valid. It definitely does not seem right for little girls to be running around in trousers with the word 'Juicy' emblazoned on the bum. I was in Bangor the other day and saw a little boy whose mum had dressed him in a pink T-shirt with the words 'Porn Star' on the chest and that is wrong on just so many levels. Come to think of it, no grown person should be wearing outfits like this either. Adults at least have a choice about what they wear or whether they choose to get dressed while drunk, in the dark, or maybe they simply have no mirror at home.

I was not a sexualized youth. I could never talk to my parents about sex in any way, shape or form. I mean really who can? They were strangely prudish, considering they ended up with seven children, which means they must have at least enjoyed a healthy sex life (I hate every one of those last ten words, it's an image I want to remove from my head). We never had that sit-down 'birds and the bees' conversation. That was not a parent-friendly topic in the Amos household. As a kid, if a woman came on TV and she was pregnant, my dad would say, 'Ah! She's had it. The harlot!' Even innocent programmes like *The Keith Harris Show* were off limits. If it came on, Dad would jump up and switch off the TV and the whole family would be left staring at the blank screen and wondering just where Keith Harris' right hand was and what he was doing to Orville the Duck. However some of my friends' parents were ridiculously open about sex and were clearly part of the hippie flower-power generation. I knew of one family that actually walked around in the nude, the *entire* family, which to me is much worse.

Didn't sex used to be a much simpler thing? You weren't supposed to have sex in case you got pregnant and then the rules were: you got married, got pregnant, then never wanted to have sex again. There is a poem by a bespectacled guy called Philip Larkin that says something like 'Sexual intercourse began in 1963 . . . between the end of the *Chatterley* ban and Beatles' first LP'. If you look at his picture then you can see why he was having trouble with the ladies, but, in any case, if he is to be believed, the whole sexualization of our society didn't even begin until the Beatles released their first album and kick-started the whole thing. That's a pretty impressive claim for the original boy band.

Then again some people say that the whole 'no sex before marriage' thing was invented by Christianity, which suggests that before that everyone was at it like rabbits as soon as they knew their times tables. If they even had times tables back then. The only thing I'm certain of is they definitely didn't have T-shirts with the words 'Porn Star' on them. See what I mean? Confusing.

Then there is the question of which side of the fence you fall on. Or to put it another way, who do you fall on? When I was growing up you were either normal or queer. With lesbians slotting into the gay category and bisexuals being, well, picky, picky, picky. These days there are an array of confusing new terms. OK? Get ready. Here we go . . .

Metrosexuality, which is presumably bumpy sex for exhibitionists on the Underground. Polysexuality, which, I guess, is sex at a second-rate university. Androgyny, which must be sex with a robot. Hopefully, a robot more like Kryten from *Red Dwarf* than a Dalek whose only mission, as we all know, is to exterminate. Then there's 'asexuality'! Even I had to look that one up. Is it like having a headache? Every night of the week? All your life? . . . By choice?! At least that's according to the online 'urban dictionary' that I use for all my vocabulary needs. I recommend it if you really want to be street-wise . . . and have no friends.

For example, the Grammy and Brit award-winning and very talented singer Adele released a song called 'Chasing Pavements'. I had no idea what she was talking about. Was I not hip enough to know this new slang term? Look it up in said 'urban dictionary' if you want to find out. Just make sure your mum is not in the room when you do it.

When it comes to sexuality, I believe you simply don't get a choice about whether you're gay or straight – sorry crazy fundamentalists of any religious order, but you just don't. Maybe you guys should just all get together and have a good old fundamentalist gay-bashing tea party. You could create a new state of hate right next to the attractive tourist destinations of Syria and Saudi Arabia: you could call it Homophobia. You could bill it to

Thomas Cook as the destination of choice for sun, sea and NO SEX.

The argument of nature versus nurture just doesn't carry any weight when you're born one of seven kids. We were all treated exactly the same, born and raised in a semi-Christian household. 'God didn't make Adam and Steve, he made Adam and Eve!' Yeah, I've heard that one and, just for the record, he didn't make Adam and Eve either. Or for that matter AIDS, cholera, cancer, war and famine. If there is a God he's got the 'Back in 5 minutes' sign up and he's having a cigarette round the back of the universe.

This attitude is why today we have to fight for rights and equality. But sometimes it can be a bit confusing. There are the LGB rights – that's Lesbian-Gay-Bisexual rights. Yes, my brothers and sisters and those still making up their minds! Fight for your rights to express yourself. Wear heels at Gay Pride while trailing a dirty feather boa, clutching a can of strong lager, and screeching 'I am what I am'. But now you have LGBTIQ rights. That's Lesbian-Gay-Bisexual-Transgender-Intersexed-Questioning rights. Wow! That's a mouthful. Now I'm down with the transgender and intersexed rights but 'Questioning'? Really? I'm not even sure what that is. Aren't we all questioning? Come on, make up your minds already! Surely, there are now more than enough options for you to choose from.

After all these years of separating everyone out into lots of different kinds of categories, when you actually go out clubbing on the gay scene it's more diverse than ever, with straight boys and girls in attendance too. The only problem is trying to figure out who to hit on. It's times like these that I feel for the 'Questioners' who must just spend the whole evening wondering, Where am I? Who am I? Beer or wine? Do I fancy that person? Do I even like Kylie Minogue?

This is not the way it has always been, I can tell you. Gay clubs of old were not the welcoming places that they are now. The bouncers used to stop you at the door and enquire: Are you gay? Are you sure? Let me see your shoes. Doc Martins? OK. I loved going straight clubbing for years; even though they had dodgy-looking blokes on the door and fights outside, they were actually less intimidating than gay clubs. The thought of going into a gay club filled me with dread so it's not surprising that I put it off until I was in my twenties.

I decided to go to the Astoria, which was one of the biggest and most famous venues in London. It was fantastic and most major pop stars, like Boy George and Duran Duran, would play there all the time. The London Astoria used to be on Charing Cross Road until it was demolished in 2009 to make way for the Olympics Cross Rail project. They barely gave any notice at all and so there wasn't any time to launch a campaign to save this bastion of London's clubbing culture. That was a crime and helped to see Charing Cross Road go from being one of the hottest streets of the nineties, filled with a weird mixture of prostitutes, petty drug dealers, world-leading theatres and artisan bookshops, into the soulless avenue of despair it seems to have now become. Just like they cleaned up Broadway in New York. Shame on them.

That first time I will never forget; it was an experience. I didn't go straight in. I walked around the block seven or eight times, head down in case anyone recognized me, until I worked up the courage to join the queue. Even the queue was a sight to see. There were lot of Mods dressed in tight-fitting tailored suits and Rocker types with T-shirts and jeans full of holes (and faces full of holes). Of course there were six-foot drag queens in scary amounts of make-up, but they were the ones on the door taking your money. I crossed the threshold and there was no going back. Well, not without losing my ten quid entrance fee.

The main dance arena catered to the tight T-shirt brigade who liked to chew the inside of their faces. For quite a few years I wondered why everyone had the same glazed expression while they danced. Call me naive but I genuinely thought they were in a trance. Back then people weren't just shouting out 'Acid!' and sporting a smiley face sticker or whistle – they were clearly 'on it' in another direction. There must have been three thousand people there that night. The music was thumping and vibrating throughout my whole body. Through the blinding light show, I could see a bewildering mixture of people. There were black guys, white guys, old and young, fat and fit. Slowly my stomach unknotted itself because here I was in a room filled with like-minded people, gay people, just simply having fun. Nevertheless, I got a drink and stood in a dark corner for at least two hours.

I was alone, but I was fascinated by what I was seeing. Guys kissing, girls holding hands, guys in drag. I was paranoid that I would be spotted in there by someone and be outed to my friends and family. It didn't even occur to me to question the reason why anyone I knew would be there in the first place. I didn't know any gay people. I thought. I got another drink from the bar and a portly gentleman of about forty-five approached me. My first impression was, Oh dear. You could be my dad. But obviously not; he was a white chap. He asked quite politely, 'Would you like a drink?' It seemed very generous as I had just bought one. But at least he was someone to talk to. We were chatting away and then out of the blue he said, 'I really fancy black boys.' I was taken aback. So in his eyes I was a 'black boy'. He didn't even know me. So I said, 'So do I.' End of conversation – he walked away.

I decided to explore the rest of the club and found an upstairs bar. Across the floor, I spotted a Latino-looking guy who was a similar age and build to me. I was smitten, but I didn't know what to do. I thought maybe I'd go for the tactic I'd just learned and offer to buy him a drink (with no mention of his race). I went up to him and said, 'Do you want a beer?' He nodded. Wow! The next thing you know we were having a conversation of sorts. It was difficult trying to have a conversation with the loud thumping music all around us. We were screaming at the top of our lungs and I couldn't understand a word. I thought he might be foreign.

After a bit of 'Pardon?' 'Excuse me?' he motioned to the barman for a pen and began writing me little notes on the back of a beer mat. Good thinking, I thought. It made sense.

'Hi. I'm Ethan!' he wrote.

'I'm Stephen. Where are you from?'

'I'm Canadian.' After a lot of toing and froing, I was relieved when he eventually wrote back to me: 'Do you want to get out of here?' A nod and we were out on the street.

I said, 'Phew. It was a bit loud in there.'

He opened his mouth and said something that I didn't understand at all. I was puzzled. My face must have changed instantly. He looked totally crestfallen and pointed to his ear where a hearing aid nestled unobtrusively. So. He was deaf. Obviously profoundly deaf. No wonder our conversation inside had been so difficult. I quickly reordered my thoughts. His disability was no reason to fob him off and I also remembered that he was totally fit.

He kissed me then and there and grabbed my hand to lead me away from the club. I followed, not really sure of what was going to happen next. He led me not far away to another gay bar in the heart of Soho called Signal, long since closed for the night. He produced a set of keys. Whatever else this guy was he was obviously well connected.

I followed him up three flights of stairs to a really plush apartment. Wow! What a result! I thought I'd landed on my feet. He could read my lips perfectly and although he spoke like someone who had been deaf from birth I could understand what he was saying. Pretty much. Even so it was definitely me who was dominating the conversation. Eventually, he held his finger to my lips to shut me up and things started heating up. Just when it was going past the point of no return, a strange person emerged angrily from a side room and stomped up to us. I was utterly shocked and more than a little bit embarrassed.

His hands were blazing in a flurry of sign language as he shrieked aloud for my benefit, 'I didn't say you could have friends here!' With not a look in my direction. 'And it's not all right! There are no parties here! Get him out!' He hadn't acknowledged me at all and poor Ethan, a grown man, looked utterly gutted and embarrassed, as if he'd come head to head with an extremely angry version of Joan Collins in her 'Alexis' phase. It was in fact as if Joan herself had burst in on the scene to have a full-on cat fight with arch rival 'Krystle Carrington' ready to pounce on her and start grappling with her curls and shoulder pads. Joan spun on her heels having thoroughly ruined everything and without much else to say (he was deaf) Ethan sadly took my hand again but this time he led me to the door.

As Ethan was walking ahead of me, I decided to at least manage a brief shout of 'You haven't got to be such a cunt about it! Dickless motherfucker!' as loud as I could, confident that Ethan wouldn't have heard me. Ethan led me back downstairs, but halfway down he turned to me smiling and let me know that he'd 'heard' what I said. I don't understand sign language but I understood exactly what he was trying to say as he pointed to his ear, then to his lips, and then, as if he was scooping the 'fuck you' out of his mouth with an expansive gesture, he did the two finger sign to the ceiling – to his housemate. He put both of his hands to his ears and then to the walls and started to shake them as if with the vibration of the curse I'd shouted before smiling at me again.

We both burst out laughing, me in my normal way, but his laugh was different. For starters it was much louder than mine and it was totally . . . wild? It was the laugh of someone who'd never heard themselves laughing and so he was completely unembarrassed by the involuntary reaction of laughter. I'm sure that if he lived to be a hundred he'd never hold his hand up to his mouth or try to stifle a giggle or guffaw no matter the circumstances. That natural laugh was so real. To be honest, we didn't get to have sex, but we kissed again there in the stairwell. Maybe it wasn't the most romantic of places but, for starters, it suited me fine.

Afterwards, we just said goodbye and I went back onto the densely populated streets of Soho with all its loudness and flashing multicoloured lights. It was completely disorientating for me. It was like I had been deaf myself and could now hear the cacophony of life all around me. I had one of those cheesy grins on my face that you see on people every now and again. The kind that says I'm really happy. If I think about it I can't even remember the name of the first guy I eventually got down and dirty with but I remember Ethan, the first guy I kissed.

16

With the advent of Facebook, MySpace and Twitter, not only has communication shrunk, but the whole world seems to have got smaller. Now, speaking with people has been reduced to a set of annoying anagrams. LOL – 'laugh out loud'. ROFLAST – 'Rolling on the floor laughing and still typing' (to me it sounds like a nasty bacterial infection as well). Or annoying emoticons like:

;*$ – I've just been punched in the nose.

<3 – What does this one even mean? That I want to kiss you with my massive pucker? That I've got enormous tits? Or an integer that is less than the third prime number? (In the end I got my C in maths A level – back when Cs were hard to get!)

Technology has changed everything in strange and unpredictable ways. For example, since when did putting a little 'i' in front of something make it cool? iPad, iPod, iPhone, iKea? OK it doesn't work for everything. iTV? The diary of iAnne Frank? No.

I remember having a pen pal when I was growing up. Whatever happened to the pen pal? He was called Gorge and he lived in Guatemala. He'd write to me regularly, telling me stories about his way of life, what he was up to, recipes for guacamole. I didn't know he was a sixty-year-old man who lived down the road. It was a more innocent time. Young people today seem to have lost the ability to write. They're too busy texting and typing, texting and typing.

Plus 'abroad' is a lot closer than it used to be. Why write to someone in France when you can just go there instead? These days globalization means that people have a different attitude to international travel. Some young kids leave school and regularly ask their parents if they can go away for a year. A gap year to see Asia or America. Back in Tooting, if anyone said they were going away for a year we'd all know what that really meant. Prison. Apart from my trip to Nigeria I'd never left the country. There had been no further family holidays of any kind. After their time in Africa, my family had no rose-tinted view of the outside world as being full of palm trees and easy living. When they originally settled in South London, even crossing the Watford Gap seemed like taking your life into your own hands. Well, actually for a black family in the sixties it was. From their point of view a trip to the Happy Shopper meant opening yourself up to a world of trouble and strife. A family holiday for them meant driving to a street we didn't know very well and winding down the window. A bit.

When I was at school we learned in history classes about the great British Empire and I'd feel a sense of entitlement. Like I had every right to go anywhere I pleased and use my British pounds to live like a king. That was until my friend Paul Baker pointed to one of the pictures in the history books and said, 'Stephen, you look more like the slaves than the conquerors.' I ran home and asked my mum and she said, 'He is right. Now go and do the washing-up. Sweep the stairs. And clean up after your sisters.'

So when I took my first holiday as an adult it was quite the momentous occasion. And the great US of A was to be the destination. I'd been seduced by the movies and I wanted to see New York more than anything. Steam rising off the subway. Steaks as big as your fist. Harlem, hip-hop and graffiti. I was a young man of twenty-four and when I had the opportunity to go I seized it.

The only reason I could afford to go on this trip at all was because I'd taken advantage of a special giveaway offer. I had seen an advertising promotion in the national press placed by the famous vacuum cleaning company Hoover. They were offering two free tickets to America for anyone who'd buy a Hoover. Henry Hoover may look like a pleasant smiley face on the outside, but I knew him as the evil clown-face laughing at me as I attempted to clean the family home. Having moved out, I now wasn't particularly interested in domestic chores and as such I was a bit of a slob in my own flat.

But when I read the advert in the paper, I could hardly believe what I saw. A free holiday to America! It was too good to be true! I went straight home from the newsagent's promising to tell my flatmate Dustin all about it when he got home. Dustin and I had stayed living together throughout university and, once we graduated, we moved in together into a flat-share in Ealing. I really liked him and I'd have liked for more, if you know what I mean. Sadly, Dustin was totally straight. When he arrived home later that evening I pounced on him as soon as he entered the room. He was used to this kind of thing by now.

Although we had both enrolled in the same polytechnic in the same year, things hadn't panned out exactly the same for us. Dustin had been a diligent student and had graduated with a good degree and already had a good job as a primary school teacher. Student life for me had meant missing lectures and going out for the day with my new-found friends. I remember the joy of freshers' week. The thrill of discovering new mates and new activities was only equalled by the thrill of discovering the student bar. We put up with its ridiculous themed nights because of the cheap alcohol. In fact, you could even bring people from outside the college as long as you had your student ID. When it became common knowledge on my street that I had exclusive access to inexpensive alcohol, I suddenly had an army of new friends from Tooting who accompanied me wherever I went. It wasn't just the cheap alcohol that made them want to hang out with me at the student bar. Oh no. They were also trying to pull the naive students (Charlotte was game).

Even though I had loads of part-time jobs as a student and a government grant, the money wasn't enough to relieve the massive expense of books, travel, accommodation and the big bar bills. Looking back, I can see how it was a crime that banks happily lured all these eager young people who had just left school with cheap credit cards and overdrafts. This is the kind of luxury that should really be reserved for proper grown-ups. I passed my degree but didn't go into barristers' chambers, and indeed had to take any and all jobs to help me pay off my vast debts.

Because of the hefty credit card bills streaming through the letter box on a daily basis, air travel was well and truly out of my price range, which was why I was so excited about the prospect of taking a free holiday.

'You'll never believe what I found out today!' I said like a puppy on amphetamines as soon as Dustin walked in the front door. I was so excited that he must have thought I was having some sort of episode. The confused look on his face said a thousand words – 'get away from me, you crazy horny bastard' was just a small handful of them. Reeling from my bizarre greeting, Dustin slowly put his bag on the floor.

'What is it, Stephen?'

'Hoover! You know Hoover?' I sounded like some kind of child with learning difficulties. I was often trying to impress Dustin but usually came off sounding a bit like a knob head. 'Hoover are doing a promotion!' I was trying to get a flicker of reaction out of his stony face; I really was obsessed with him.

'So?' he said, nonchalantly.

I was dumbfounded. I was not expecting this lame non-committal response and could barely contain my frustration. 'Hoover are giving away two free return tickets to America. We could go to New York.'

Dustin's face once again showed no excitement as he paused. 'Do you have to buy a Hoover?' he said, matter of fact. Imagination was not his strong suit.

'Yes! But you get a free holiday to America,' I repeated sarcastically.

'Well, they're not free then, are they? There's got to be a catch, Stephen. There always is,' he replied in a pedantic tone. 'You're an advertiser's dream victim, Stephen. You get caught up in the hype. Remember when you bought those global hyper-colour T-shirts and magic-eye posters? All you got was a terrible headache and neon-green sweat patches. That was not an attractive look.'

'This is totally different. It's a win–win situation. Do you have any idea how much tickets to America are?' I didn't know how much they were but they had to be cheaper than a Hoover normally costs. Unconvinced, Dustin picked up his bag and headed to the kitchen.

'We don't need a Hoover,' he said as he went. This exchange really floored me. I couldn't understand why Dustin wasn't excited by the prospect of going to the States with me. Plus we definitely needed a Hoover. I knew Dustin was well travelled by my standards, but surely this was a once in a lifetime opportunity. We had to get in there quick! I thought it was a no-brainer. Go out, buy Hoover; get tickets, go to America; job done. And I told him so.

I followed Dustin into the kitchen. 'Well, how much is a bloody Hoover then?' I shouted dementedly. Probably not the best way to get him onside.

Dustin looked at me sternly. 'Stephen, we DON'T need a Hoover. You probably read the advert wrong. You're going to end up buying a Hoover and getting a free ticket to York. What kind of an idiot would give away two free tickets to America for the price of a vacuum cleaner? Next you'll be saying you've found a bag of magic beans.'

'We can just get a basic one, it doesn't have to be top of the range,' I suggested.

'It's just a scam for people like you,' he replied.

People like me? I thought. He thinks I'm a gullible idiot just because I bought a pet rock the year before. Now I had to teach him a lesson. 'OK, I'll get the Hoover. A top-of-the-range one. I'll use it everyday. I'll go to America and take someone else,' I said confidently.

'OK,' he replied. That had backfired horribly in every way.

The next morning, after a restless night of dreaming about what I'd do in New York, I was in the queue of my local Argos store. If you've never been to an Argos, think of it as a poor man's bookies; you go in, flip through a catalogue, write down your choice, take it to the counter to await your number to get to the top of a little screen and reach poll position. After around forty minutes, I was getting impatient with the large dole-like queue system. It was only then that I noticed most of the other customers were collecting Hoovers! Some large, some small and some extra-large. I began to feel nervous. Would I get mine? Will they run out of stock? Will there be enough tickets to America to go around?

My number was called; a lump appeared in my throat. Heading up the counter, I could see a long red box saying 'Hoover'. It was emblazoned with 'Flights to America Offer Inside'. I handed over a fistful of crinkled pounds and grabbed the box off the lady at the collection counter. I had my new vacuum cleaner.

When I got home, I eagerly ripped open the box like an overexcited child on Christmas morning. I was on a mission to find my golden ticket and I barely took a second look at the suction device. It was a real *Charlie and the Chocolate Factory* moment when I saw underneath the contraption written in bold: *'How to claim your 2 free tickets to the USA.'* There was a telephone number to call. Never has the purchase of a vacuum cleaner been a moment of such excitement.

I still wanted Dustin to come with me, but I didn't want to come off needy and desperate by bringing it up again. So at six o'clock, when he normally got home from college, I made sure to be nonchalantly vacuuming the hallway carpet. Dustin came in and ignored me as I extravagantly Hoovered around the front door. He went into the sitting room and I followed dragging the vacuum cleaner body behind me. Dustin turned on the TV and made a point of ignoring me in spite of the hurricane of noise coming from the vacuum cleaner. It wasn't until I actually began to vacuum the socks on his feet that he looked up. 'Oh, so you got it, did you? Glad to see you're putting it to good use. If you want to vacuum something else, my room's a bit dusty. You know where it is.'

Switching off the machine, I was about to resume my persuasion tactics when the voice of Trevor McDonald came from the television screen. 'Hoover, the great American brand of suction vacuum cleaner, is threatened by bankruptcy following an ill-fated promotion offering residents of the UK free tickets to America. Extraordinarily, the offer was made to anyone who purchased the vacuum cleaner in question. And there seems to have been no catches or caveats to the offer. Heads appear to be rolling in the offices of Hoover Europe amid claims the company will not be able to honour its no strings attached promotion. Kate Adie has more.'

The television cut to a woman wearing a flak jacket and helmet being buffeted from all sides by a massive crowd trying to get into the Argos superstore. Bits of Hoover and Hoover boxes lay destroyed and mangled in the background of the shot. It looked like a war zone. 'See!' I said, pointing to the television screen. I turned around but Dustin was already at the phone, dialling the number at the bottom of the Hoover box. 'See!' I said again with a satisfied grin.

'What have you been doing since you got home? Just sitting around and waiting for me to come home to Hoover my socks? What if we're too late?'

'Oh. It's *we* now. Who's the gullible fool? Ay? Who is a sucker for hype, ay?'

Dustin looked at me like I was being a total idiot. 'Great, Stephen. So, you're right and I'm wrong and we may miss out on tickets to America because you didn't pick up the phone the minute you got home. Are you satisfied?'

Actually, I was satisfied. To be proven right is always something that satisfies me even if in the end I lose out on something. Some call it pettiness, I prefer to call it justice. The phone rang and rang, but Dustin hung on the phone like his life depended on it. I did what I could to help out by making endless cups of tea for us to slurp. Then I started doing impressions of famous American stereotypes, trying out my Harlem walk or pretending to be a

Texan oil baron and acting out famous scenes from *Dynasty*.

As the minutes stretched into hours, I started to make us margaritas – a very poor version of a margarita, bearing in mind I didn't have the correct mixes and I wasn't a cocktail barman. It was more like bitter lemon and vodka over crushed ice. I tried massaging Dustin's neck, which was getting stiff from having the phone cradled against it for so long. I made us dinner. We ate it. I even started to vacuum the stairs just to pass the time. Finally, after about two hours, Dustin screamed out, "Turn the vacuum cleaner off! I've got through!"

I raced downstairs and listened in with Dustin as a very harassed-sounding woman spoke through the receiver. 'Hoover free flights promotion. Can I help you?'

'Yes! We've bought a Hoover and we want our free flights.'

'Where would you like to go to?'

'New York!' we both cried in unison.

'We're a bit oversubscribed to New York. How about Alabama?'

'In the Deep South? We've been on the phone for hours. New York, USA is what we want,' said Dustin calmly.

'And we have a brand-new Hoover right here!' I shouted down the line. I switched on the power and waved the hose at the receiver. 'Hear that? We want to go to New York!'

'Yes, sir. You and about thirty thousand other people. And if you think holding the end of a Hoover up to the receiver and shouting at me is going to make me go any quicker then think again. I've already been here for fourteen hours today trying to satisfy our valued customers. Believe you me, sir, I'm doing my best, and I don't even know if I'll have my job at the end of the week. Maybe you'd rather I put you back on hold.' Her voice was teetering between icy-cold hatred and the soft squidgy tremble of a nervous breakdown.

Dustin hit the end of the Hoover away from the receiver and glared at me. 'I'm really sorry about my friend. He's just very excited about the prospect of leaving the country. He's been kept indoors most of his life due to being a hyperactive idiot. Please believe me when I say we really want this trip to New York.'

'OK. What's the point in hanging up? There's only another thousand of you lot waiting to talk to me. Well, give me the serial number on the Hoover box. And there are a few conditions. Firstly, you have to pay for all your own flight taxes. That's £200 for the pair. You'll be covering your own expenses and we fly you in and out of Philadelphia International. It's an hour and half out of New York. Don't complain because that's the best we can do. You've heard of flying coach? Well, because of costing issues you guys can only have one piece of hand luggage allowed. Checked bags are extra. What's your date of birth?'

'Sixth of September,' Dustin shouted down the phone.

'OK. The dates of your travel can be the sixth of March, the twenty-fourth of December, or the fifteenth of January.'

'That's not very convenient because I have work on the—'

'Take it or leave it!'

I could see Dustin trying to think quickly, then his face went pale. 'I can't go, Stephen. Not on those dates! You'd have to be homeless or a student to make those sorts of dates.' He looked desperate.

I grabbed the phone off him. Damn. The only people I could think of whose dates of birth I knew off by heart were members of my family. By now Mum had had one more child, Elizabeth, and then finally stopped having kids and so the Amos brood had stabilized. I started counting them off on my fingers. Stella wouldn't be able to make it as she had a well-paid job in a laboratory. Albert was just getting married – he'd never come.

Cordelia, Andrea and Elizabeth were still at school and Hoover wouldn't issue tickets to minors. Chris was the only option. Chris the too-cool-for-school teenager had just turned eighteen. He'd be doing his A levels in March, so that was out. December? That was Christmas. But January was a possibility.

'I can make it for the fifteenth of January no problem. Print the tickets.' Chris wasn't even twenty-one so how would we go drinking?! Whatever. I'd bought the Hoover and I was going to capitalize. The Amos brothers were going to hit the States. I gave his name and date of birth and sure enough the tickets arrived within a week to my flat. I later discovered that Hoover had lost £25 million as a result of this promotion and they had to sell the whole company to Whirlpool.

I hoped that Chris would be able to come with me in January. He might be at university or could even be working, but knowing him it was quite possible that he'd be doing neither. There's a six-year age gap between me, Stella and Albert and the younger kids and something odd had happened to my parents in that time. The pressure put onto the younger kids by Mum and Dad was nothing compared to what we'd lived through. Those babies could get away with stuff that would have been unthinkable for us. The chances of Chris being forbidden from going on holiday to America aged eighteen was probably less than Mum and Dad giving me a hard time for taking the trip at twenty-four.

I might have to sack off the first week of work in the New Year but that shouldn't be a problem. I figured I could just say that a distant relative had suddenly died. One of the good things about having a huge family is that there is a long cast of characters who can have an accident befall them. This time it was going to have to be my sick great uncle who had suddenly died with a funeral to arrange and attend – I couldn't use my grandmother again. By this time she had suffered so many calamities forcing me to take time off that in the employment agency I was affectionately known as Little Red Riding Hood.

For me, I was going to America and nothing was going to stop me! My next stop was visiting Grosvenor Square to sort out a visa. This was in the days before it was easy to go to the US by filling out the visa waiver form online. I had to queue for hours at the embassy to get my paperwork in order and they asked me a lot of odd questions. Like, was I a Nazi? That seemed like an off question since my Aryan credentials are somewhat lacking. It's not easy to get through an interview like that when you're a natural joker and I had to bite my tongue more than once.

I wonder at American intelligence agencies. I mean, why just come out and ask a question like that? Couldn't they have tried to be a bit more sneaky? Like: What is your opinion of toothbrush moustaches? Or a how about a multiple-choice word association game to trip you up. Maybe: If I say the word 'tikka' do you think of a) Chicken, b) Lamb or c) Swas? Or how about: If I say the word 'anschluss' do you reach for a) A Kleenex tissue, b) U2's acclaimed seventh album or c) Austria? I think things have tightened up since 9/11 but count yourself lucky that you don't have to go to the embassy in Grosvenor Square any more. It was pretty imposing back then, but it's a lot more imposing now they've installed vats of boiling oil on the roof ready to be chucked down at any invading foreigners.

I did manage to get the visa and on the fateful day of travel I arrived at Heathrow Airport with Chris in tow. Though Chris was a well-rounded young lad he was still six years my junior and I had a sense of responsibility because I was in charge of a minor. Plus my mum had said that she would kill me if I allowed anything to happen to him. There's nothing like the threat of death from someone who'd lived through the Biafran war to focus the mind. I looked over at Chris, with his shoes untied and chewing gum, and resolved that we were going to have an amazing time. He may have been my second choice of travelling companion, but he didn't have to know that.

17

'NEW YORK! NEW YORK! It's a helluva town!' So the song goes. And it really is a non-stop madcap place of pure mayhem. When Chris and I arrived at the immigration desk, after all the rigmarole in the UK of queuing up at the embassy to get visas from a surly official, the guy at the desk was surprisingly friendly and welcomed us with a big smile. We got our bags and headed for the taxi queue, where immediately as we came out of the terminal I saw my first American arrest. A Latin American taxi driver (maybe he was driving without insurance?) was stopped by the cops and face planted to the ground. I looked at Chris and if we had ever doubted that New York was basically a film set blown up to city size, we were now under absolutely no illusion.

When we got our cab the driver was a black guy who had his hair intricately braided into a dollar sign. He turned to me and Chris and said, 'Where you going? The 212? The island?' We looked at him like he was totally mad. 'Are you guys going to Manhattan or what?' We nodded and he pulled off at speed. We immediately hit unbelievable traffic and, just as we were getting used to the idea of sitting through a long and expensive hold-up, the driver just powered over to the hard shoulder and drove down it at about eighty miles an hour. As four lanes of stationary traffic honked and shouted abuse at us, in the back of my mind, I started thinking of Nigeria.

I am no fearful driver myself, but was totally terrified and clung to my seat for dear life as we careened around on the half-muddied dirt track next to the motorway. The driver tuned the radio to full blast hip-hop and Chris shouted out, 'Oh my God! Is this Hot 97?'

'Sure is. You heard of it?'

'Of course! It's in all the best hip-hop tracks. "Hot 97 so I guess I'm flexible. Twee! Twee!"'

'KRS 1?'

'Stop that Chris!' the older brother in me snapped. I had no idea what they were talking about but apparently Chris and our cabbie had just launched into a rendition of a famous song by some rapper. That's New York for you. Even the radio stations are world famous.

In Manhattan itself, from bridges to streets to museums to squares, you literally see one incredibly well-known sight after another. The cabbie dropped us off at our hotel off Broadway and immediately gave Chris his beeper number. 'Beep me 911 when you want to go out and I'll show you the clubs.' We had arrived in the Big Apple and it was a friendly place.

I'd done my research before heading over there so that I could fit in. But I found out that I couldn't possibly fit in because Americans have no idea of what to think of a black British person. They haven't got a frame of reference. They're used to the Harlem style and a certain attitude. They were confused by me. I went into a local coffee shop and simply said, 'My good man, I'll have a cappuccino please.'

They were like 'Say what?!' Gesturing in disbelief to the other waitresses in the shop to run over to us. 'Alopecia! Get over! Anaconda! Get over! Now say it again!'

I said, 'My good sir. A cappuccino, please.'

'Whoo-ee! It's Geoffrey from the *Fresh Prince*.'

New York is different to London in many ways and one of them is the attitude. People are overall a lot more friendly than they are in England. For example, in London, if you see someone dressed in a Lycra catsuit roller-skating along with a boom box belting out Kate Bush in Hyde Park, you shuffle quietly away. In New York there'll be like 'Yo! Way to go. More power to you!'

In the UK, people tell you that you can't do stuff but in the States they say, 'Yes! You can!' And it was in New York that I met someone who would completely change my life for ever. They managed that by simply telling me that I could do something that up until that point I'd never even considered.

My one contact in New York was Michael. I had met Michael back in London and we'd developed a good friendship that had sadly been cut short when he went to live in America. Michael lived for the theatre and, more specifically, he lived for musicals. Since seeing *Cats* with Fola when I was fourteen years old, I hadn't gone back to the West End to do anything other than visit a pub. But when I met Michael and he said, 'Stephen! We're stepping out!' you couldn't say no.

We had gone to see *Five Guys Named Moe* in the West End, which had been a real toe-tapping sing-along (of course Michael's friend had been in the show). On another occasion, I didn't consider it a date but Michael might have had other ideas, we went to see the amazing Chita Rivera, star of *The Kiss of the Spider Woman*. This time we were in the front row and I could actually have reached out and touched the leading lady.

Michael's love of the theatre, the stars, the razzmatazz (is that even still a word now?), meant that he had a burning desire to go and live in New York, where he is to this day. How he got to live there and get a job as an assistant at an actors' agency remained a mystery. You could visit America quite easily back then but to secure the elusive green card to work there was virtually impossible. I never asked but he was irrepressible and so he told me how he'd done it. He'd married an American girl that he'd never even met! His boyfriend, though, was lovely.

Chris and I spent the first few nights with Michael and we saw the sights of the city. Two shows a night was normal for him and in the middle we'd go to the local steakhouse where ribs were the size of your head. Luckily for me, visiting Michael in New York at the same time as us was his best friend from London. It was a lady named Delphine Manley.

Chris and I met her one morning at Michael's apartment. The apartment was everything I expected from a central Manhattan tenement block. It came complete with those wrought-iron metal fire escapes at the back, which are straight out of *Cagney and Lacey*. Of course my first suggestion was to re-enact an episode by running up and down those stairs playing cops and robbers and shouting 'Hold it,' in a Bronx-style accent.

At nine o'clock in the morning, this was not warmly received by Delphine, who was staying there too. She was a well-spoken, slight girl who was pretty, talkative and full of positive energy. I hit it off with her immediately and shortly she suggested that we all go out to a local bar that was serving a New York brunch. This was otherwise known as an all-you-can-drink margarita brunch. (Proper New York margaritas.) Brunch. It was the first time I'd ever heard the word and it stuck. Forget the Irish, the Scottish, the Ozzies and even the English – the biggest drinkers in the world live on the East Coast of America. I made Michael's place my first stop of the morning, where I'd use the word 'brunch' euphemistically, frequently and mostly inappropriately.

'Who's for brunch?' I'd say at 10 a.m, while pouring tequila shots.

'You're really funny, Stephen. You should do stand-up.' Delphine dropped the bomb.

'What? Don't be silly. I've never even seen a stand-up show,' I replied.

'I think she's right,' quipped Michael.

I was taken aback. People said that I was funny, but I was still foreign to the world of performance and I had no idea what a stand-up show would entail. Not only had I never been to see any live comedy, the stand-up that I had seen on television was definitely not aimed at me. In fact I couldn't relate to most of it. Mainly portly, middle-aged men from the North in dinner suits – all telling black jokes, Paki jokes, gay jokes and mother-in-law jokes. The audiences may have been guffawing, but I didn't belong to that arena. The only time we ever watched comedy at home was if Lenny Henry was on and I said so.

'No,' Delphine continued. 'There's a whole new wave of alternative comedy in the club scene, it's really growing.' I looked quizzical. 'I'm going to open a comedy club in London. I've been running them at university,' she said.

'That would be amazing!' shrieked Michael, clapping enthusiastically.

'And I want you to be the resident MC,' Delphine continued while smacking down her margarita.

'What's an MC?' I enquired, genuinely wondering if it had anything to do with MC Hammer.

'You know. The host. The guy that introduces the comedians.'

I racked my brain to recall any stand-up I'd seen on TV that had an MC. Nothing came to mind.

Delphine went on. 'Just think about it. Let's exchange numbers and get together in London.'

With that, we exchanged contact details and Michael was genuinely excited and pleased that a connection of sorts had been made. I put Delphine's details away in my wallet, nestling between the remaining few dollars I had to spend and my credit card (which was now for emergencies only!) and I thought no more of the conversation.

Fun times in New York were over far too quickly and I was back in London, with my younger brother safely in tow. I almost lost him altogether on our last day when we had a huge argument. I can't recall what it was about but I was probably suffering from the overprotective older brother syndrome and was telling him off over some trivial thing. We were riding the subway together still smarting from the argument and the next thing I knew, he'd disappeared.

Good. At first I was pleased that he'd fucked off because that meant I had won the argument and therefore been proved right! But after a little while I panicked. He may have stormed off in a teenage huff but I had no idea how to find him. He'd gone and I wasn't even sure if he knew how to get home. The only thing I was completely certain of was that I was not leaving this country on my own.

I'd witnessed lots of people haunting the underground network and drinking from mysterious brown paper bags while shouting maniacally. At the time, New York was not a safe place for a young foreign black man to go out in alone. And after seeing the overzealous arrest of the taxi driver at the airport, I was always on the lookout for trouble. Several times I'd crossed the street when I saw an undesirable type walking towards me. It was mostly the uniforms and the badges that were offputting.

Honestly, I don't know what I feared for the most: the loss of Chris if I couldn't find him or the loss of my life, when my mum found out. Losing one son in a bizarre accident is one thing, but killing another son as punishment? I didn't know if Mum would go that far but it was a definite possibility. In a panic I got off the carriage to begin looking for him. As the train pulled away, I looked behind me for a split second. Chris was still in the same carriage as before but had just moved to a seat further away from me. We both realized what had happened but it was too late. The train had moved on.

I decided to catch the next train as I hoped he would get off at the next stop and wait for me like any naughty brother would. When we slowed down at the next station, peering out of the window, I saw Chris, and a huge sense of relief washed over me. The look of relief suddenly drained from my face however, because my train did not stop. I had inadvertently got on a fast train on a different line heading straight for the airport. Disaster!

This was in the days before we all had mobile phones, so I had no way of contacting him. Besides we were underground, so they wouldn't be a lot of use anyway. Chris couldn't be relied upon to know where we were staying and I didn't think he had any money to get a cab either. There followed a distressing three hours of two lost Englishmen in New York playing a game of cat and mouse chasing each other round the subway and the city. It was a nightmare, but on the plus side I now know the Manhattan underground transit system really well.

He wasn't at the hotel that we were staying at and finally, in despair, I went to where Michael lived. I'd done all I could and, as I got off the train, I was practising what I'd say to Mum, while also thinking of what to write in my own farewell note. But there on a bench by the exit I saw a familiar and exhausted face. While I had been frantically retracing our steps Chris had sensibly found his way to the stop that we always got off at for morning brunch. It took three hours out of our day to reach this point but at least we were both going to stay alive. We laughed, embraced and neither of us could remember what the argument had been about in the first place.

This was just one of the many stories that I regaled to Dustin when I got back to London. For weeks afterwards, I could see the envy in his eyes. I'm pretty sure that had he known how much fun we'd have, he would have taken some time off work or even gone halves with me on the Hoover. However, he didn't say anything and I respected that. It fits in with a never apologize, never admit you're wrong way of thinking.

A couple of weeks later I had the pictures from our trip developed. Now that does seem like an outdated thing to say. To the kids reading this: look it up! That's how we did things in the olden days. Some of the pictures were blurry and others had just my brother's finger on them. That was the problem with old rolls of film – you paid a flat fee to get them processed but out of a typical twenty-four exposures, eight could be put straight in the bin.

The handful of photos that did come out were a great talking point for the next few weeks when mates came round to visit. I think they only put up with me sharing stories about my trip to New York because they also shared my enthusiasm for New York brunch. It was during one of these boozy evenings that the phone rang and it was Delphine on the end of the line. She called totally out of the blue and, to be honest, it took me a while to recall who she was. She suggested demurely that we meet for coffee but I don't drink coffee and suggested a proper '. . . drink! Like the ones we had in New York!'

'Then we can go to a comedy club too, so you can see one in action for yourself,' I agreed and we arranged to get together that Friday night. I was intrigued as to why Delphine thought that I could be a good MC. Dustin thought she may be a little bit arty and crazy perhaps or even simply after my pants, or, more accurately, what lay beneath.

We met in a pub in Putney, South London and I arrived early, looking earnest with notepad and pen in hand. When Delphine arrived, she was all smiles and acted as though we'd not been apart since New York, which by now was nearly a month ago. I was taken aback at how much she believed in me, bearing in mind she had never seen me on-stage before. I couldn't help thinking it was a great risk to open a new comedy club with some new bloke at the helm, who had never, repeat never, ever, done it before.

'You'll learn as we go on,' she said encouragingly.

'I hope so,' I replied sheepishly.

'You can help me set it all up, get as much out of it as you can. Come on, let's go upstairs, the show's starting,' she continued.

All I could think was, What the fuck. What I have I got to lose? You don't know until you try. When we went upstairs, I witnessed live stand-up comics on-stage for the first time. The amazing thing was I didn't hear a sexist, racist or homophic word uttered. I was hooked.

The next week I saw my second ever stand-up night at the Big Fish Comedy Club in Richmond from the unique position of actually introducing the acts. All of my best mates turned up and laughed uproariously at everything I said. I thought I was a dab hand at this. The second gig didn't go so well. The crowd in Richmond could be unpredictable. Sometimes it would be mixed and sometimes (the worst times) it would be the posh locals. It was my second gig ever and I stood there trying to banter with a bunch of people who just weren't having it. I didn't really have much material back then and I was just riffing with them when I said, 'Ladies and Gentlemen! While I'm standing here talking to you, all my mates . . . are robbing your houses.' One woman put her hand up (very posh for a comedy club) and said, 'Excuse me? But isn't that rather racist?' I said 'No . . . What are you saying? How do you know these friends I'm talking about aren't white.' And I won them back. Most of the best gags come to you when you go with the flow and that was one of the first lessons I learned in comedy.

These days, comics start out doing five minutes, then ten minutes, then twenty. Once they've found their comedy voice through doing rehearsed sets then they can start compering, where you have to play it fast and loose and be in the moment. But I did it the other way around. I started out compering. So I never had to rely on scripted material and never had that white heat moment when you forget your next link or your punchline. Likewise, I've never had that long drawn out painful death when no one likes you or your material and you've got no option but to power through twenty minutes while getting nothing back from your audience (except undiluted hate). It was a baptism of fire, but it suits me to riff and play around with people and their expectations of me. I'm glad that I never listened when teaches or parents told me to sit down and shut up because now I'm never lost for words on-stage and I like it best when I can chuck the rehearsed set out the window and just have fun.

So just like that the Big Fish Comedy Club was launched upstairs in that pub in Richmond. Our budget was non-existent, so just like when you are decorating your house, mates and favours were called in. The Big Fish theme was extended to give the venue an identity and it was decorated like an underworld cave in the sea, with nets, plastic fish, seaweed and shells. Dustin got his class to do a project making fish of all different shapes and sizes to be hung around the venue. I told him how creative I thought the idea was; others may see it as free child labour.

I never for one second thought of it as a potential career opportunity, but Delphine and I worked together over the next couple of years and, before I knew it, there were four more clubs called Big Fish dotted all over South London and I was compering four nights a week. To this day, I am eternally grateful to this woman, who came into my life and led me down this extraordinary path. Delphine quite literally turned my world around. And to think how differently things would have turned out if I hadn't got that bloody Hoover!

18

BIG FISH SEEMS LIKE a long time ago and I quickly moved from being a compere to being a regular touring comedian. I love travelling around the UK but it's not all glamorous by any means. It's actually a lot like being a long-distance lorry driver. We both know the quickest route from Ipswich to Lowestoft at three in the morning. We both know exactly where all the petrol stations on the M1 are. We have an uncanny ability to tell exactly how many miles we've still got in the tank when the petrol gauge reads zero. When we see an empty Coke bottle we see a mobile toilet.

It can actually be quite boring constantly trawling up and down the motorways, but you can find comedy in the most unexpected places. For example, I recently saw a motorway sign about a mile outside Oxford that made me laugh. It said: 'Emergency Toilets 30 Miles Ahead'. Excellent news! That's just the sign that you're praying for when you're weighing up the dangers and merits of pulling onto the hard shoulder and relieving yourself three feet away from passing articulated lorries.

When you're travelling all over the UK, you develop a fondness for some places. Lowestoft is one of my favourites. Other than at the theatre, they seemed to have no actual people living there. Why would they? When I was there last, I read in the local paper that traffic in the centre of town was being suspended for a day so the council could have a terrorist bomb attack drill. I peered out the window at Lowestoft and thought, It looks like they've already been.

Seaside towns can be the most fun places to visit. Even better than Lowestoft is Rhyl. Affectionately known by the residents as the 'wart of Wales', you may not have heard of it, but it's only a stone's throw from Liverpool. A Molotov cocktail toss from Chester. A baby hurl from Anglesey. And a dog lob from Wrexham. Don't blame me – that's how they measure distance in Wales. It was in Rhyl that I took a stroll down at the beach and found a shop that, honest to God, sold nothing but golliwogs. Hundreds of them. I wasn't going to stand for that: I bought the lot and I set those fuckers free.

And you get to sample the delights of local cuisine when you travel around a lot. I was in Belfast and I went to the local chippy and got a big fish supper.

I asked innocently, 'Do you have any tartare sauce?'

The man behind the counter looked at me like I was from the future. 'No. But we do have Lilt.'

At the gig in Belfast, I got on stage and before I'd finished my first joke someone had placed a pint of Guinness at the front of the stage. Everyone was shouting, 'Down it! Down it!' By the time I had 'downed it', nine more pints had appeared on stage. I actually got a bit drunk and was mortified when I had to run off-stage in the final five minutes to take a hard-earned piss. 'Music on please!' I shouted to my tour manager and ducked off stage. To add to the horror, I'd forgotten that there was no toilet back there. I had to run back on stage and grab a handful of the empty pint glasses. This turned in to an imprompto cue for the audience also to go to the toilet or the bar. An unplanned interval, much to the delight of the crowd.

I've been lucky enough to play at our best music festivals. I went to Glastonbury and when I got there they told me that I'd have to camp. I looked at them and said, 'Me? A tent? On the ground? I don't even caravan.' So they found me a hotel nearby. I've got say that I didn't go there for the music. I went there for the extra-curricular activities and for the party. At about three in the morning, I was in the comedy tent and my friend comes up to me looking like he was tripping. And not the light fantastic. He said to me, 'Steve? Steve? Am I inside or outside?' I said, 'You're inside.' He said, 'Steve? Is this a coffin?' Being a good friend I said, 'Yes! He asked, 'Steve? Am I dead?' I replied, 'The name's God!'

Not every gig goes well. For example, I did a show in Portsmouth Jongleurs a few years ago during which I inadvertently started a race riot. Jongleurs is a very well known and successful comedy club chain. They used to be everywhere and for a long time they were the bread and butter for a jobbing comic. I am grateful to the team there for the huge amount of effort, support and work that they gave to not only me but many other comics that passed through. Some of those comics are now household names.

However, Jongleurs was very well known for attracting a tough crowd due to the disco that followed the comedy. Hundreds of hen and stag parties frequented it and munched down on the legendary fried chicken platters as they drank jugs of beer. The comedy was a precursor to a night of over-drunk single men dancing to very loud 'Billy Jean', hoping to pull in the magic hour between two thirty and three in the morning. That time of the night when your brain is computing the amount you've spent, the number of drinks you've quaffed and the attractiveness of the girls still at the venue according to the law of diminishing returns.

So I went on stage and did my best material. I used to do a bit where I'd pretend to be my dad and talk to the audience in a thick Nigerian accent. Everyone was having fun except for one table near the front. They were obviously a family as there was a mum, a nan, a man and his girlfriend. As a stand-up, if someone isn't laughing and everyone else is, you naturally fixate on them. I was determined to make them laugh and focused on the younger man who seemed particularly morose.

'You, sir, wearing glasses. Have you found Jesus? The Lord gave you vision at a limited rate. You defy him by wanting to see more?'

Other people in the venue were definitely laughing, but I was getting nothing from him. After a few more prods, his mum piped up and said, 'Save your breath. He doesn't talk to niggers.'

I was gobsmacked and I braced myself for the audience reaction. Thankfully, the chorus of boos and disapproval was deafening. But the mood in the room had definitely changed. I could feel all eyes on me and I could either walk off stage angry or deal with it. I decided to engage him in the only way I knew and so I said, still in my Nigerian accent, 'Why say that? You could be my son. Well, obviously not. You're a white boy and this isn't prison.'

To which he replied: 'Learn how to speak properly!'

In my most clipped voice, I said, 'I think you'll find I can speak better English than you and your father's father.' I didn't want this to escalate any further and was about to call it a night when an Indian guy in the front row decided to take over my cause for me.

'You ignorant bastard!' He threw a full jug of beer over the offending man's table. I raised my hands to diffuse the situation but suddenly there were tables and chairs flung everywhere and I watched in horror as two hundred people fled for the tiny emergency exit.

I had the best view of all because, although I'd unleashed the situation, I was strangely immune to the riot that was erupting. The factions remained in the audience, fighting it out amongst themselves. That was until the mother of the guy in question came running up to the stage and started shouting at me, 'You don't know what you've done. He just got out of jail on licence this morning. Now he'll go back in. I hope you're proud of yourself!'

I didn't know what to say and thanked God when another comedian who'd been on the bill, named Ava Vidal, came out to save me. Ava is a stunningly beautiful and very tall black woman who takes no shit. What's more she used to be a prison guard and so knows how to do a chokehold when the occasion demands it. She ran on-stage and managed to keep the four feet around us free from mad racists before bundling me to a safe distance.

'Shall I get her, Steve?' she asked nonchalantly.

'Erm. No. Do you think I should go out and finish my set?'

'I don't think so, Steve. Thank God I've already been on. Who would want to follow that?'

When you're on tour you've got to learn to take the bad with the good. One night you can be playing the Hammersmith Apollo and staying in a fancy hotel and the next you can be playing an obscure town in Norfolk and staying at a B&B. But it's sometimes the smaller towns that have the best crowds. In fact, the last time I played King's Lynn I was actually saved from having to spend the night in my car because of the kindness of an audience member.

King's Lynn's got a beautiful theatre called the Corn Exchange in the main square and it was full that night. My production team were booked into a hotel, but the show had gone so well that some of the locals invited us out for a drink afterwards. I was on a high after the gig and so I agreed, and one dodgy Wetherspoon pub, a kebab shop and an unmentionable club later, we were the last ones out on a Saturday night in King's Lynn. In London you never get to an hour when there's nothing left to do but in King's Lynn that hour is about two in the morning and so we decided to head to the hotel.

One of the new friends we'd made from the gig offered to help us find the hotel, but when we got there we found that it was already closed for the night. Our slightly inebriated minds took a moment to let this fact sink in. Having expected to head there straight after the gig, we'd not checked in and had no keys to the building. After half an hour of banging on the door, my production manager started looking worried.

'I can't believe they've locked us out!' I shouted with one more bang on the door.

Just then our new friend said, 'You don't come from around here. This door may look locked to you Londoners. But it's not King's Lynn locked.' And with that, he used his shoulder to barge the front door. The next thing you knew three men were standing looking slightly panicked (probably) and slightly unsteady on our feet in the foyer of the hotel.

I had foolishly hoped that we'd find a friendly (if deaf) night porter on the other side of the door with a set of keys in his hand who just hadn't heard our loud bangings. Unfortunately, our troubles weren't over and, although we'd made it into the hotel, we still couldn't find our room or a key to get into it. We sat forlornly in the empty bar and my production manager set to calling all the other hotels in the area, but they all claimed to be full. Once more we resigned ourselves to sleeping in the car and started to discuss who would take the front seat for an uncomfortable night. However, once more, out new friend came to the rescue.

He said, 'What are you looking so miserable for?'

'We're stranded.'

He went to the bar, pulled two pints, and said, 'You're not King's Lynn stranded!' And he promptly left the building.

'Hang on. He said we're not stranded and then he totally abandoned us here,' said my production manager before taking a sip of his beer. 'Oh well.'

We were still sitting and miserably drinking our beers when we heard a racket and our new mate emerged looking very pleased with himself. 'I'm back! Drink up! I've got a plan!'

We went back outside with him and he'd brought a car. 'Get in!'

'Here. Are you sure you've got a licence?' asked the production manager. 'I don't want you doing anything illegal.'

'It's not King's Lynn illegal!' he announced and we all hopped into the back of the car and he drove us back to his parents' place. Hurrah! Saved! We'd be able to bed down for the night and maybe get breakfast in the morning too. I readied myself for a good night's sleep as he parked up and led us into his back garden. 'Here we go. We can sleep here.'

I looked around and the yard was covered in sheds, overflowing with rubbish, and a couple of dilapidated and rusty-looking caravans.

'Sleep where?'

'In the caravans. I've got the keys.'

'Hang on. Sleeping in a caravan. Isn't that a bit trampy?' I asked

'It's not King's Lynn trampy!'

That night we slept very comfortably until his dad came out at eight in the morning with the dogs to check who'd broken into his back yard. So there you go. You never know what you're going to encounter in this job. One day it can be luxury and the next day it can be a caravan. But who cares? As long as you meet nice people on the road I'm not precious.

We're lucky in the UK because we have the best city in the world for live comedy. London's good, but I'm talking about Edinburgh, which hosts the world's greatest arts festival. When I first went up to Edinburgh in the mid-nineties it was during a time when success at the Fringe could make a big difference to your career. My first experience was doing the Big Value Comedy Showcase at the Cafe Royal with great mates Will Smith, Carey Marx, John Gordillo and Lee Mack. A couple of years later I thought it might be worth a go doing a solo show up there so I secured a 7 p.m. slot in the Pleasance Courtyard and gamely took the coach up with all my stuff. When I stepped out of the bus station into the New Town at seven in the morning, I was amazed at how stunning the city is. The New Town is all Georgian terraced houses built around grand squares on a beautiful grid system. The Old Town is all gothic spires and winding cobbled streets more suited to a horse and cart than tired feet.

I had a room to perform in, but not a room to stay in because Edinburgh accommodation rates normally triple in the month of August. Thankfully, my friend Gavin had told me that I could stay at his place, but since he wasn't arriving for a day or two, I'd booked into a youth hostel. It wasn't an eight-bedroom dorm – I splashed out – OK, yes, it was a four-person. It was pretty grim, but I figured it was just for a little while and I could handle it. As a jobbing comic, I was in fact quite used to making hundred-mile journeys for £50 and sleeping in cars or on couches to make ends meet without complaint.

I don't want to sound precious, but I'll never stay in a youth hostel again. I once asked Arthur Smith, who's been going up to the Fringe since it began, why everyone came up year after year and he said, 'Well. It's not for the food, deep friend haggis will never be a big draw. It's not for the drink, Tennent's, although that doesn't stop us from drinking it.' He pondered. 'There's always been a lot of sex.' And he was right. At least there was in the hostel I was staying in.

I'd gone out for a couple of welcome-to-town drinks with some friends, but I had decided to be sensible and made it back at a reasonable hour. One other person in the dorm room was not so civic minded and at about midnight a really drunk bloke stumbled in, and he'd brought a date with him. Let me ask one thing of you. When you've met someone nice and they say to you 'Your place or mine?' and 'their place' is a dorm filled with three other people please just take their number and suggest meeting the next day for coffee. Don't go back with them to have awkward sex on a bunk bed and keep everyone else up listening to your performance.

In fact it was a lot like a really shit Fringe show because it lasted for an hour and everyone was praying for it to end after five minutes. We got to listen to him struggle to perform in a hostile room for what seemed like an eternity. When you're making love and it lasts for an hour and you're sober then that's great. When you're drunk 90 per cent of the time it's because Cupid's arrow can't find its target and the bow is just getting chafed. When he'd finally finished, we all breathed a collective sigh of relief; I got up, opened the door and said, 'Fuck me! After that *I* need a fucking cigarette.' And didn't return.

If you've been to Edinburgh you may have noticed that all the different rooms at the main venues have quirky creative names (so you think) like 'Cellar' 'Closet' or 'Dungeon'. When you get there you realize that these are just descriptions of the rooms themselves and very accurate they are too. There are so many comics trying to find places to perform that every broom closet, gym and basement gets converted into theatrical spaces.

My show that year was in the Pleasance 'Attic' and it was literally a hot and sweaty attic up a set of winding back stairs that you needed a map to find. I was incredibly excited on the night of my first performance. My name was up on the wall, I'd had fliers printed and my announcer called out my name. 'Good evening, ladies and gentlemen! Please go wild and crazy for Mr Stephen K. Amos.' I leaped on stage, arms outstretched, ready to accept the applause; I looked down and there were five people in the audience. Four lost-looking punters and a reviewer.

The show was a character piece, during which I played four people – it was so traumatic that DJ Bug-Eye is the only character that I can actually remember. I'd not thought it out very well and so during the three costume changes I had to make I hadn't come up with a convincing in or out for me to get off-stage. Nor indeed had I brought up any music to play during these frequent intervals. So the audience sat in awkward silence as I rummaged around behind a curtain putting on wigs and jackets.

Unless you're very lucky, your first solo Edinburgh run is bound to be an uphill struggle. I was desperate for people to come and see my honed show, but I resolved that if fewer people turned up than could fit easily around a pub table then we'd just go to the bar downstairs instead. Edinburgh isn't a big city, but they have the most comedy savvy audience in the world and millions of pubs. With so many hundreds of thousands of people seeing shows and talking about it over a drink afterwards, what really makes or breaks a show is the word-of-mouth effect.

Getting a good buzz going around your show is vital, but when you first go up to Edinburgh you think it's all about getting that elusive review. The local paper publishes dozens of them every day and they even had a Page of Shame, which was a page of one-star shows of total terribleness. But there are so many reviewers up there that one year a very successful comic friend of mine managed to get a five, a four, a three, a two and a one star review all in the same season. That's why I have a never got my head around reviewers. People who think they can publish a critique of an art form they generally have never attempted themselves. As Andy Warhol said, 'Don't count the stars, count the column inches.'

I went up to Edinburgh every year for ten years in a row because it's such great fun. It's a comedy summer camp for big kids and it's even a kind of comedy workshop where you learn a lot. It's the first place that comics have to perform an hour show, because in clubs around the UK, unless you're the compere, you can quite happily get by on doing tight twenty-minute sets. Plus there's an unwritten rule that every year you go to Edinburgh you have to present a new show, so without the Festival to spur you along you might just stop writing.

It's not just your own gigs that you do. Lots of comics take part in plays as well. I remember one year there was a production of *12 Angry Men* showing and I was desperate to be in it. It's about a jury deliberating the fate of a black defendant so I thought I was quids in to play the defendant. I got my hopes up. I got my agent to call them. I was beginning to get a bit hacked off that no one was getting back to me so I went out and bought the play. The whole thing takes place in the jury deliberating chamber and you don't even get to see the black guy. It's supposed to be an artistic look at the dynamics of racism, and no black guys are involved. Typical!

It's not just comics up in Edinburgh. You get all sorts of performers and living works of art pounding the streets in August. The world's most pierced woman can often be seen on the Royal Mile fighting her way through the street performers. The circus normally comes to the Spiegel tent where you can see seriously sexy and astonishingly lithe artists getting up to no good. One unforgettable year *La Clique* ruled the festival from there, with their performances nightly followed by a full-on swing dance club-night spectacular. You'd get in free if you came in fifties dress and the troupe would always come down on the floor to jive-dance with the audience until the early hours.

There are some unforgettable people and venues that you encounter year after year. The Gilded Balloon holds its own as one of the big four venues and Karen Koren has been running it since the beginning. She always manages get the rowdy crowds and comics into her venue with the world-famous *Late 'n' Live*, her rambunctious after-hours comedy club. If Scotland had a hurricane season then she would be the hurricane. You'd see her in the old Gilded Balloon, the one that burned down in 2001, at *Late 'n' Live*, drinking a glass of white wine and shouting, 'Get off! You doughnut!' with the rest of the boys. It's probably because comedians are creatures of instinct and habit that they keep coming back to be heckled year on year, but also it might have something to do with the fact that Karen never disappoints to set up the best bars at the festival. It can turn into a land of booze hounds and cougars until the wee hours and, when nobody had the money to pay for the drinks, I'd hoped Karen would forgo the bill and put it down to karma.

The Gilded Balloon was my home away from home for years and Karen made me the resident host of *Late 'n' Live* on Sundays for years. Some extraordinary things happened on that stage, but I'll never forget losing at a near-naked wrestling match with Daniel Kitson. I still can't believe I lost.

It was outside the Gilded Balloon that I had one of my favourite Edinburgh experiences of all time. After the original Gilded

Balloon suspiciously burned down, Karen moved it to new premises in a quirky gothic castle on the huge Bristo Square at the top of the Old Town. It is notable because it's very picturesque, its toilets stink to high heaven (to prohibit cocaine use perhaps) and it has a very overactive fire alarm system.

There was one time when I was halfway through my set and the alarm went off, demanding noisily that everyone evacuate immediately from the building. The next thing you know a thousand people were outside in the vast Bristo Square, milling around in the dark and lamely wondering if and when they'd be allowed back into the venue. I had been on a great roll in my show and I just didn't want to stop, so I got an upturned crate and continued with the gig out there in the square.

The Gilded Balloon has dozens of performance rooms but most of them hold about two hundred people maximum, but now the square was bursting with the audiences from all the shows that had been running in the building. So I had a huge crowd to play to and it was bloody brilliant. Using all of my lungs, I kept the show going to thousands of people and when the other comics saw what I was doing they wanted in on the action. That night we turned Bristo Square into an al fresco free-for-all comedy club featuring Daniel Kitson, Jimmy Carr and Mitch Benn among many others.

In Edinburgh, people sing and tell stories at late-night impromptu gigs. Fights and pints are cheerfully exchanged in a city that has turned the 'local' vibe to perfection. Arthur Smith still does his midnight city tours in spite of the rain and the odd arrest. I saw a dwarf on roller skates being pulled along by his cock. I saw a couple strip and leap into the sea and swim. I saw a seagull fight a man for a chip and win. You see a lot if you keep your eyes open. And if you do well you could get the chance to play at other international festivals.

After Edinburgh, the best festival going is the Melbourne International Comedy Festival in Australia. What makes it amazing is the audience. Australian audiences are very similar to UK audiences. They are savvy, smart and know how to take the piss out of themselves. Even the rednecks know they're redneck and play up to it. Over there they call them 'bogans' and no matter who you are you'll be amazed at what they come out with.

I went to a typical Ozzy barbecue last time I was there and the topic of gay marriage came up. I braced myself when the bogan host stood up. But he surprised everyone when he said, 'I don't see the problem with gay marriage. I think it's great. Because if you're gay and you're married then you can bash each other! And no one ends up in court!' He went on, 'I don't understand how they can use religion as a reason to ban gay marriage. Religion is full of holes. Take the anti-abortionists. I was listening to talk radio the other day and this priest comes on and says, "Abortion is morally wrong." I thought, I'm not having this so I called up the station and spoke to him. I said, "Say your daughter is raped . . . I mean theoretically." They cut me off, Steve, but that's the kind of question I'd ask anybody.'

Then his wife piped up. 'Don't you know that's an inappropriate question to ask a priest? What were you thinking? Priests aren't allowed to have any children!'

'Oh yeah. I heard that the Catholic Church doesn't want priests to have kids. But that's just because when a priest dies they don't want any kids to inherit their wealth and their houses. So the Church can just take it back. This has been going on for years and years. Don't you know how rich the Church is? Of course, they are. Cos property prices have gone up a lot since the sixteenth century. Think about it.' Australians are wonderful people.

There are a handful of other good festivals too but for some reason none in the States. I don't know why, but maybe it's because Americans are really polarized and a joke that one person finds funny in New York might get you shot in Alabama. So Americans travel all around the world to see comedy and you always bump into big groups of them.

I met an American couple at a show and afterwards they come up and they were *lovely*; they get a photo and an autograph, but after a minute of two they start looking uncomfortable and trying to get away from me. I said to them, 'Why are you in such a hurry?'

'Stephen! We're seeing eight shows today! You're number five and we've got to get to the next one. I half expected them to shout: Go! Go! Go! USA! USA! USA!', before diving into the crowd and army crawling to the next gig.

That's one kind of American. The worldly kind. There is also the other kind who look a bit bewildered being outside of their own country. A bit like deer caught in headlights. I ran into a couple of Americans like that in Edinburgh a couple of years ago. They were easy to spot as Americans because they were large and they were wearing bin bags. A note of advice to the world: Scottish people who live in a country where it rains all of the time will prefer to get wet rather than wear a disposable poncho and I recommend that you do the same.

I couldn't help but have a bit of fun with these Americans. It was a few years ago, when I had my face on the side of some of the black taxicabs to advertise my show. The saw me, recognized my face and came up to me, pointing up at the glistening spires of the Old Town and said, 'Excuse me, sir! Excuse me! Up there in the distance. Is that Edinburowow Castle?'

I couldn't help it. I said, 'No, my dear lady. That is Gotham City!'

They said, 'Oh my God. How do you know so much?'

I said in my finest Nigerian accent. 'Lady, I am the last king of Scotland.' And went to hail one of my cabs. The moment was somewhat ruined because, did the fucking cab stop? No, it did not. Some things never change . . .

19

SOME PEOPLE ASK ME WHAT it's like to do comedy live on stage night after night and all I can tell you is that it's a completely unique experience. Not everyone can do it and you have to have a thick skin. You can't do it in front of a mirror at home and it's not the same doing it in front of your friends or family. To get behind a microphone and build a rapport with a room full of strangers who don't know who you are is a nightly challenge and it's a sink-or-swim kind of situation.

If you survive the feeling is like nothing else in the world and you're high as a kite for hours afterwards. If you fail there is nothing that can get you out of a venue more quickly – and I can guarantee that there's nobody in the club who'll want to run after you to rub your back and save your feelings. You're just a bloke on stage who thinks he's funny and the crowd can warm to you or they can chew you up and spit you out unceremoniously.

There is a common misconception that heckles make a show. Believe me, any good comic worth his salt does have a set that he would like to deliver heckle free! In the UK, people love to get stuck into you but thankfully you are the man with the mic, and with experience, should have the ability to put a heckler down like a ton of bricks. If you can survive a good heckle then you can get an audience back on side. However, sometimes heckles are funny and can totally get under the comics' skin.

I was doing a gig in York and a newbie act was on stage. He wasn't having the best gig of all time. The crowd weren't going for it and, to make matters worse, someone had brought a newborn baby to the gig. Nobody was laughing, and all that could be heard in between the flailing comic's attempts at gags was the sound of this little baby gurgling and sniffling. Eventually, he said to the crowd in exasperation, 'Who brings a newborn baby to a gig?' and someone else in the audience shouted, 'Maybe she's trying to get it to sleep!' Everyone laughed their heads off and so did the comic. But he never gigs in York any more.

You can't let the crowd take control of the performance because if you give them a bit of power then they (of course) misuse it. There was one particularly harrowing time at the Edinburgh Fringe when I witnessed a performer crumbling into a thousand pieces. Admittedly, this occurred at *Late 'n' Live* which is well known as a no-holds-barred beer-throwing gig and many comics go there after their own shows to heckle each other.

Some totally unscripted and memorable things have happened during that show, but I was once witness to an event that nightmares are made of. I suppose it must have started as one of those 'good idea at the time' moments that spiralled out of control. A journalist had decided to have a go at doing *Late 'n' Live* and then write an article about it afterwards. It was a publicity stunt. But it's the sort of thing that's going to really get up the nose of other comics. The fact of the matter is, stand-up's not easy and not anybody can do it. A great comic just makes it look easy, and there's a difference.

So this guy was going to do the comics' comic gig and he let it be announced beforehand that he was trying out an experiment. A bolshy move, but actually kind of an insult to the whole profession if you think about it. It would be like me going up to a journalist and saying, 'What? You're just pushing bits of paper around all day. Any dickhead can do that.' (Something I would never do.) Unsurprisingly, nobody gave him the slightest break. He'd decided to jump into a shark tank after cutting himself just to get them into a feeding frenzy.

So picture the scene. This excited journo steps onto the stage with a piece of paper in his hands and announces that he's going to try out a few jokey jokeys from a list (he'd probably meticulously prepared). He gamely launches into his first gag and he gets absolutely nothing. Props to the audience for even allowing him to get out his first attempt at a joke but by jokey jokey number two the whole crowd were shouting out, 'Boo! You're shit,' 'Fuck off! TAXI!' and the best of all: 'You killed Diana!'

As many people would react when faced with abuse from a room full of strangers, he didn't handle things well. You could actually see any mojo that he ever had drain out of him, and he started channelling the persona of Ed Miliband on ketamine. Any normal person would have fled for the exit as fast as humanly possible, but he actually tried to continue with the list. There were cries of 'Not the list,' and the perverse encouragements of 'Yes! The list!' as the smell of impending death seized the hyena-like crowd. At one point, a truly surreal moment, he started to utter animal noises as if his human consciousness had retreated right back into the base of his brain (who could blame it) and his monkey brain was coming to the rescue.

He managed to keep his head high until he did something that you shouldn't do. He called an audience member a fat bastard. Not a serious insult by any means but there's an unwritten rule that says you can't swear at people in the crowd. You can say anything you like to humiliate an audience member. You can embarrass them in front of their friends so badly that they'll never live it down and their wife and children will leave them and change their names. But you can't swear at them, especially if you're getting no laughs. That's the biggest no-no. After all, they've paid money so the crowd really turned on him: the compere came out to try and take control of the crowd. But the journalist had not got through his full set and so the compere had to fill in the dead time before the next act. Guess what the hot topic of conversation was? The Scottish weather? The differences between men and women? No, it was how unutterably shit this guy had been.

In the fracas somehow the stage had got wet, probably from a water glass hurled at the poor journalist, who was hopefully being consoled in the backstage. Someone was going to have to clear it up. After fairly brutally ripping the journalist to shreds and on the audience's insistence, the compere said, 'Shall I make him come out and mop the stage?' The stage manager appeared with a mop and the barely recovered journalist came back on stage to mop up.

Crowd can be inventive in their bastardry. There is a gig that happens once a month at London's Comedy Store called *The Gong Show*. You have to get on-stage and survive five minutes without being gonged off. Rarely do real comedians try to do this gig because it's not really about material; it's about the audience baiting and heckling people. There is normally a final at the end where anyone who actually makes the five minutes goes head to head and a winner is announced. This gig is such a sadomasochistic experience that often the participants are a bit mental.

One time I was watching this comedy cock fight and the audience noticed that we were getting towards the end and only one person had made it to the five-minute mark. The savvy ones amongst them realized that they would be denied their final blood match and so decided to get behind someone to give them a proper end game. But they didn't choose someone good. They waited for the absolute worst train wreck of a gagsmith to take to the stage and laughed and applauded wildly whenever he said anything or made the smallest gesture. Looking into the comic's eyes, you could see that he knew he was being toyed with as his gags became weaker and weaker and the audience went wilder and wilder. By the end, he would have begged to be booed off and put out of his misery. It was like a firing squad shooting a condemned man in the foot and shoulder only because they wanted him prone for the final killer bullet.

If a heckle is funny, I'll run with it; or if you're challenging a statement the comic has made then fair enough. But often a heckler is just a drunk trying to be the centre of attention. Crowds used to be a lot worse than they are now. About ten years ago, I noticed a distinct change in audiences and comics alike. Gone was the spark of originality and a steady influx of sexist and homophobic jokes started to be delivered under the guise of irony. There is nothing wrong with telling jokes about race, gender and sexual orientation if the intent is clear. You have to be trying to make people laugh and not just do someone down. But at this time in the clubs a lot of the intent behind the jokes was getting blurred and it gave the audience the right to shout out outrageous stuff with the excuse that 'it's only a joke'.

I was at a late-night comedy club when a female comic, a good friend of mine, took to the stage. It was Friday and the audience were tired and intoxicated. Standing at the back of the room, I watched as the MC introduced my mate. The cheers were notably half-hearted but what happened next made my eyes pop out of my face. Back then the typical male to female ratio in club audiences was 85:15, while the ratio to female comics on a regular bill was even less.

Before she even reached the microphone stand a gruff voice shouted out from the crowd, 'Oi, ugly, I can smell your cunt.' It was the worst heckle I had ever heard, but the audience reaction surprised me even more. It was met with a chorus of massive laughs and applause, as though it was the most brilliant, intelligent heckle ever told. My mate walked right off the stage shouting, 'Fuck you! I don't need this!' That was a long time ago and thankfully things have changed since then. For one thing, these days, she says, she washes it before going on stage.

It's not so nice when people decide that they can get away with something that would be considered a hate crime outside of a comedy scenario. I once was playing a gig in the East End of London and someone shouted out, 'Oi, darky! I never knew, I never fucking knew, that black people were funny!' That took me back, but I wasn't going to get defensive. I just said, 'Some of us ride bikes. Have been known to ski. Work with rudimentary tools.' All I got in return was 'Ay? Wassat?' He didn't know what I meant. So I won that one.

When an audience is sitting in the palm of your hands it is a fantastic experience because you are making a connection with them. It's intimate and you interact with them and they interact with you. It's like a table-tennis match and the audience is on your side because after all they want to laugh and play with you too. Just don't forget that you can rehearse a set until it's perfect but you need to be able to chuck the whole thing away if something happens in the room that you weren't expecting. And when that thing happens and the gig gets spontaneous, that's worth a million one-liners.

A lot of unusual characters make the decision to become stand-up comedians and often people who are extroverts on-stage are introverts off-stage. They can be quite deep, often very intelligent. I was travelling with a well-known comic recently and a fan came up to him and, after talking to us for a minute, he said to the comic, 'You're not very funny in real life.' This comic just turned to him and said, 'Mate! Get a grip! IT'S AN ACT!' Maybe the fan thought he was being cute, but he got the whole concept of stand-up comedy wrong. As I said before, it's only meant to *look* easy.

For the most part my on-stage comedy persona is very similar to my off-stage persona, but every performer lives a bit of a double life. Comics' lives are the opposite to other peoples' lives. We go to clubs and bars to work. Our busiest times are in the evenings, at weekends and at Christmas. In fact, when I was first starting out in comedy, my dad was the first to notice that I was keeping very strange work patterns. I knew he'd hate the idea of me doing comedy, so I actually started out by telling him that I was a minicab driver. However since he noticed that I would always dress up in smart suits before leaving, plus I didn't have a car at the time, I knew this fiction wouldn't last for ever.

'Stephen. What is going on in your life? Where are you going dressed like that night after night? Do you really drive a taxi?'

Eventually, I sat him down, took a deep breath and said, 'Dad. You're right. I've been living a double life . . . I'm a stand-up comedian.'

He said, 'Phew! I thought you were gay!'

20

IN MY OPINION, LONDON is the best city in the world. The old buildings that crowd the centre are a reminder of its glorious past. The nightlife is good enough to give you a hangover for a week and it was on the arts scene that I first performed as a comedian. If you come to London then you've got to spend some time exploring it, but to me the best thing about the capital is the diversity of the people. Nowhere else in the UK or maybe even the world can you find so many different nationalities and cultures all living pretty much in peace and side by side. New York in the USA has a similar mixture of peoples, but over there people seem confined to specific areas. So you've got Latin barrios, black neighbourhoods, white enclaves, Middle Eastern districts, gay villages and Chinese quarters. Here in the UK it's a mash-up of cultures.

Today my local chippy is owned by a Chinese couple who just shout at each other all day long in Cantonese as they fish pickled eggs out of the jar. The local Chinese takeaway is run by an Indian who plays loud Bhangra in the kitchen. My local Indian serves omelette and chips! Maybe Londoners have an identity problem. They don't know quite who they are supposed to be. I was walking down the high street the other day and I heard a voice shout out:

'Yo! Steve! My bredren! I saw you on *Live at the Apollo* last night! You was bad, yo!' And that was a white kid talking.

These days, on the surface, London can be a pretty tolerant place. You can hear a dozen or more languages being spoken and there are shops and restaurants that cater to every race colour and creed. I was once ordering a kebab from a Kurdish restaurant in North London and they had 'sheep's member' on the menu. I'm guessing it had something to do with getting into some kind of secret society and nothing to do with eating the cock of a sheep (an animal with questionable hygiene that gave us the word 'dingleberry').

If you really want to get a taste of the melting pot that is London then the best place to look is the world-famous London Underground, where you can see all these different people running around getting to work in the morning or going home at night. The Tube is very deep but don't be afraid of the morlocks; we call them 'buskers' and although a lot of them look like they haven't seen natural light for years they don't live in the tunnels and they don't eat people. In fact, the buskers are a highlight, so if you want to catch a fully grown man playing the ukulele half a mile underground then come to London!

They even considered getting stand-ups to entertain people on the Underground just like the buskers. But this would never work out because there is a Golden Rule that no one is allowed to talk once they've paid their fares and gone through the turnstiles on ground level. If you talk, no matter what you are saying, then everyone immediately thinks that you are a madman. Even if an Underground employee says that the train is delayed or that you have to evacuate because of a fire, you look at him askance thinking, What mental hospital have you escaped from with your bright orange high-vis jacket and walkie-talkie?'

This doesn't mean that people don't do other wildly inappropriate things on the Underground. Many women seem to think that a hot stuffy underground train whizzing around at thirty miles an hour is the perfect, most sanitary place in the world to apply make-up. I recall watching in complete amazement as one woman managed to put on lipstick, eyeliner, mascara and also brush her long flowing locks on a particularly bumpy Northern Line train. She was completely oblivious to the fact that she was moulting like a rabid dog all over anyone within a mile of her and that she resembled an evil clown by the time she got off. Of course, no one said anything to her because of the Golden Rule.

This tradition of total silence means you can have a moment to yourself, can read a good book or play my favourite game, which is trying to guess the life story of the people standing next to you. Or, if you get bored of that, then you can try to figure out who would eat who first in the event of an accident and everyone getting stuck on the train. Or you can try to guess who would hook up with whom in case of the same event. Or if that's not your cup of tea, then you can play another good game which is trying to read the free newspaper of the person sitting next to you.

There was one time when I broke the Golden Rule of not talking to people on the Underground and sure enough I met a mad person. It was when I was just starting out doing stand-up and I was travelling to a gig and trying to read the newspaper of the person next to me. It's a challenge because although the papers are completely free and are thrust into your face as you're entering the Underground, passengers, once they've got them, treat them like their last will and testament. However, I've built up many years of practice and have it down to a fine art. You have to keep your face forward and totally expressionless. Don't move any of your arms and legs and try not to breathe too hard. Basically, act like someone's injected Botox into your brain. Then you have to imagine that your eyes are on stalks and slant them over as far as you can to get a glimpse of the headline story.

I only managed a sly glance before the man next to me grunted and shuffled awkwardly, as he tilted his free paper further away from me. It must have been my psychic presence alone trespassing on his front page that he was disturbed by. With so many people squashed together on the Underground there is a lot of psychic energy flying around. You share air, elbow room and sometimes it even seems like you are sharing thoughts with your fellow passengers. It was then that I heard a laugh opposite me. I looked up and caught the eye of a very attractive black girl. She looked down as our eyes met, but was still grinning broadly.

How long had she been watching me? Why didn't I spot her earlier and did she now think I was the worst newspaper rubbernecker in history? I kept her gaze, while trying not to appear like a weirdo (not an easy task). She was smartly dressed and had a closed book on her lap. I wanted to see if this lovely early-twenties beauty had a sense of humour and I saw the opportunity for a joke. I opened my eyes as wide as I could and stretched my neck in an exaggerated way, pretending I was trying to read the cover of her book. Bingo!

Tossing her head backwards, she laughed again, this time using her hand to cover her mouth to try and stifle the sound. Good manners, I thought – so unlike the heathens who think nothing of sneezing, coughing, yawning or eating on the Tube without covering their mouths. I liked her dress sense too. Normally, everyone on the Tube is sweaty and irritable because they're still wearing their overcoats, hats and scarves from outside. The cute red hat and matching red gloves she was wearing made me think she was style conscious. In hindsight, it should have made me suspicious that this stunner seemed to be dressed for the hot Tube and not the freezing weather of the street.

I was trying to keep her laughing and so my moves got a bit more jerky and exaggerated. Rarely has this sort of thing happened to me. A random encounter that grows into something more just like that? It was like something out of a silent movie and I was getting a bit carried away by the attention she was giving me. I hadn't felt this way about a woman in ages. People often ask me if I'm attracted to women or to men. I think that's a stupid question. A better question would be – are men or are women attracted to me? Secretly, I hope both are, but when I find someone sexy who is giving me the eye then I'm going with them (if they'll let me).

I've had relationships with women and with men, but if I have to choose one or the other, these days, I have to say I'm gay. There's no two ways about it. All my brothers and sisters know, but I didn't come out to my parents for years. In fact, I'm not sure that I've exactly come out to my mum even now. Her attitude to sex and sexuality is just to ignore it completely. If my mum were to walk in on me having sex with a bloke, I'm sure that she'd say something like, 'Stephen isn't gay! That boy he is having sex with. He is the gay one!'

Nevertheless, I was completely mesmerized by this girl and I'd completely forgotten about my neighbour until, with a sharp huff, he flicked his newspaper straight. Maybe he thought with all of my jerking movements I was in fact having a seizure. By now he wasn't reading the paper any more and was also giving my lady the eye. This is a ruse used by many Tube riders. Have a book or newspaper handy, pretend to read it while trying to look up a skirt, down a blouse or in any other direction to catch a glimpse of the people in front of you. Failing that, try looking at the glass reflection opposite to check out the people next to you! It works every time.

The lady in red was still smiling and my grin was wider than the platform at Tooting Broadway. Eye contact is one thing, but if we'd been closer together then I could have made foot contact. Our chemistry was unmistakeable but I was too embarrassed to make a move on the packed Tube. Irrational anxiety set in. The kind that only rears its head when you fancy someone and don't have the guts to do anything about it. What if she gets off next stop? Then I'd have blown it for sure. Then more panic. What if we get to my stop? I may have had a gig to get to but at this point I was willing to sack it off. I thought to myself, I'll stay on the Tube and get off when she does. I'll make it natural looking, if that's possible. Only a strong infatuation can make you look at a total stranger and think, Yes, I'll definitely follow you home.

The Tube slowly juddered to a halt when we pulled into the next station. I was wound so tight that when newspaper man stood up to leave, my body reacted instinctively and I began to rise too. My mistake made for a weird musical chairs moment and I sat down again sheepishly, feeling pretty foolish. However, right on cue, my new girlfriend laughed. Yes, she must've thought I was playing another joke. Get in there, Stephen. Saved from the jaws of disaster.

With newspaper man off the Tube there was a seat free next to me. Now, here we are at a crossroad. I like girl, girl like me, there's a spare seat next to me. Sometimes I wish that girls would just take the initiative. No sooner had I finished my lust-crazed reasoning when the stunning girl moved across and sat next to me. I got a lump in my throat.

'Hi,' she said. 'I'm Marcia.'

I opened my mouth and broke the Golden Rule – 'Stephen, nice to meet you. Erm, are you off out somewhere?' What a stupid question. Did I really think that she just went round and round the Circle Line all day? But I was thinking on my feet and figured that at this stage I ought to be polite to make up for the neck jerking and mad facial expressions that had been my method of communication so far. From a distance, our silent love mime had been quite endearing; continuing it close up could indicate mental health issues. As it turned out my mental health wasn't the problem.

Then Marcia dropped the bombshell. Taking her hand off the cover of the book, she continued, 'Can I interest you in the Lord?'

It was then I noticed the book's title: The Bible. Growing up, my parents used to discipline us the old-fashioned way: by using religion. By which I mean they used to beat us with a copy of the Gideon Bible. Plus, I'd had to endure endless evangelical church services in Nigeria, so I really don't like organized religion much at all. With one simple sentence she'd let me know that the whole sorry charade so far had just been an attempt to coerce me into being converted to the bloody Good Book.

I looked her up and down again and suddenly her beautiful outfit made sense! What a temptress! My previous question turned out to be surprisingly apt as it looked like she must indeed just ride the Tube lines looking for people to preach to about God. What a manipulative, poisonous, Venus mantrap. Plus she'd lured me in and distracted me from the fun of reading a perfectly good free newspaper.

'I, er, I haven't really given it much thought,' I replied, feeling deflated in the extreme and studying the Tube map intently, counting the stops until I could get off. If anyone had witnessed our sweet exchange a few moments before – boy, they must be laughing now.

'Well, maybe now is the time for you to give your life to Christ.'

I couldn't ignore her because she was now sat next to me. I looked longingly for another seat to move to but now, predictably, the whole carriage was full. 'We have many Bible classes in this area, can I invite you along?' That was about as far away from my idea of a dream date as it was possible to get.

'How did you find the Lord?' I asked. That question shook her right off balance. Good.

'Erm. A bit like this really, someone stopped me on the Tube and I was hooked.'

I saw an opportunity to quiz her and I went for it. 'Well, what if that person was a Muslim, or Hindu or Jewish?'

'What do you mean?' Her face had now visibly changed. The pretty smile was gone.

'I'm just saying, maybe that person caught you at a bad time. You could have been a Hare Krishna or an atheist.' (And going back to my flat with me right now, I silently added.) 'What if that person had been a ticket inspector? You could have been a convert to working on the London Underground by now if you'd met the right person at the right time.'

She sat back further in her seat and her hand once again covered the Bible. 'There is only one God. Through Jesus Christ I will be saved from the many temptations I meet on the way.' She retaliated in that painfully rehearsed way that you get from people who have found religion and are now using it as a shield against all argument or sensible discussion. 'I know what you're doing.'

'I'm just asking a simple question,' I protested.

'No, the devil works in mysterious ways. You have come to challenge me, to test me.'

'Isn't it God who works in mysterious ways?'

Before I could finish she interrupted abruptly, 'You are the devil. I suggest you mend your ways and find the Lord.'

The Tube arrived at the next stop and, with precision timing, she was up and heading for the door. I expect she was just going to catch another train and find someone else to convert. As the doors opened, she turned and gave me a look that could have removed paint from a toilet wall. I had been unceremoniously dumped and condemned as the devil within minutes. This city is full of surprises, some good and some bad. On the surface, London is a tolerant and permissive place. But watch out when you get on the Underground. Here there be morlocks.

21

THERE'S SOMETHING ABOUT London's West End that's just fucking cool and I'm very lucky to have spent six months of my life playing there. And playing is just the right word. Live theatre is like live comedy and nobody's in it for the money because almost nobody makes any. But people keep turning up to work because the community of actors, producers, directors and technicians are so full of affection for each other. It's a surreal night-time world consisting of dilapidated dressing rooms, painted scenery made of plywood and late-night bars. The whole strange backdrop takes place under hot bulbs and heavy foundation.

When they asked me to take a role in *One Flew Over the Cuckoo's Nest* in 2004, I initially said no. Why would a stand-up comedian like me, getting by very well using my own words on-stage, want to surrender half a year to performing a script written by some American? I'm pleased to say that I am easily led and I took up a residency at the Gielgud Theatre with a bunch of my best friends for a season.

The play is about a mad house and the director had decided that they would cast all the crazies from London's red-hot stand-up comedy circuit to play the inmates. To add some star power to the production, Christian Slater and Frances Barber were cast in the lead roles and the result was very successful. Being battle-hardened comedians we wouldn't have cared if John Gielgud himself had been resurrected to play the lead and I think perhaps our anti-star-struck attitude allowed the Hollywood and West End glitterati to let their hair down.

The show was baptized at the Edinburgh Festival where the home-made careless irreverence of the world's greatest arts festival gave the show the rocket fuel it needed to hit the ground running when we came to London. The Edinburgh Fringe is a place where anything goes and we took some of that misrule spirit with us to the West End and ruled the streets while the show was on. Barber and Slater were like a Royal Family with an unusually large court of funny man (and woman) jesters.

I remember the first night in the Gielgud set the scene. I played one of the nurses, which was a good speaking part (although I played one of the bad guys and not one of the clowns). At the curtain call, Christian Slater and Frances Barber accepted the rapturous applause. But, as a kind of joke, my best friend came running down to the stage from the gods baring a bunch of flowers. Christian went to take them, only for my mate to cheekily brush him aside and give them to me instead! I have to say that even though I didn't steal the scenes I was in, that night I certainly stole the show (sort of).

Being a comedian I didn't take it all that seriously and was just having fun. I was unaware of the serious rules of the theatre. You have to turn up an hour before the performance; you can't drink until the final curtain; you can't leave the theatre; and you mustn't wear your costume outside. All of which are sackable offences. I managed to commit them all in one afternoon, when I decided to go and meet my friend during the interval at the Samuel

Smith's pub next door. I only realized something was wrong when the company manager came running into the pub shouting 'Amos! Get back on stage!' I'd actually missed my cue. I had to apologize to my fellow cast members using the Tannoy system backstage. I couldn't resist the chance of another funny. So I said over the system, which relayed to every dressing room, 'Ladies and gentlemen, I wish to apologize for missing my entrance as I had visited the pub. I can honestly say this may never happen again.'

Still, for six months, that crummy rundown pub was the de facto West End green room. Once it became known that Christian Slater and Frances Barber were frequenting it, suddenly you couldn't move for people like David Schwimmer, Patrick Stewart, Dennis Hopper, Donatella Versace or whoever else was in town for the night. You'd catch them at the bar trying to figure out if Alpine Lager for a quid could really be a good idea to order in public (if you've been to a Sam Smith's pub you'll know what I mean). I think Donatella took one look around at the hookers and ancient winos who were the traditional customer base and turned it into her shabby chic collection for the spring.

Playing in the West End meant that suddenly we all had membership of all the members' clubs and we abused our new-found stardom to the max. When you're with famous actors you can pretty much get in anywhere and do anything. We even found those few strictly exclusive bars that are open very late and don't have a barman. They call them 'honesty bars' and they just expect you to take what you like and leave the money. I was so impressed that I left a tip. I wrote on a piece of paper 'Get a barman!' as I tucked into a fourth bottle of champagne.

Most of the cast being made up of comedians, we even put on a special late-night comedy show involving all of the actors, including the serious ones. Christian was nervous about it and so one of the other comics cheekily gave him one of my lines to use just before he went on stage. I don't think he even had time to read it beforehand. He marched on and said, 'I love performing in front of you good people. But really, this isn't all that. What I really want is my own TV show. But the BBC have a very strict diversity policy. Apparently, I've got to wait for Lenny Henry to die first.' Now, coming from me, that's a very funny joke. But coming from Christian Slater it sounds like he has an unnatural urge to murder an innocent black man, who he'd probably never even heard of. Still, we couldn't help laughing.

Probably the most rewarding part of doing the show was getting to do the matinees for school groups from disadvantaged areas. These youths had never been to the theatre before and during some shows you'd hear them talking or texting on their mobile phones. After the performance, the organizers would arrange for a Q&A session, which to be honest was quite painfully forced. You know the kind of ill-thought-out event that none of the actors and none of the kids really wanted to do. You could see the teachers prodding the students to ask Christian Slater questions and we'd get stuff like 'How do you keep your uniforms clean?' and 'Did it hurt at the end when they electrocute you?' They clearly had no idea who I was as one of them asked me, 'Hey, can you do the Ezekiel bit from *Pulp Fiction*?'

The whole thing was an unforgettable experience with hundreds of people grouping around the stage door every night hoping to get autographs from Christian or Frances. We'd go out clubbing together and I remember there was almost a riot when I took Christian Slater to Heaven, London's biggest gay club. He was totally mobbed. But fair play to him, he took it all in his stride and posed for pictures with the regulars. It didn't do me any harm bringing him there because I had honorary VIP status for the night.

Years later, I still look back on that time and can't really believe it happened. After it was all over, most of us comics went back to our day jobs: making people laugh in clubs. It was quite a head shift going back to the Jongleurs comedy circuit. I didn't mind because when we were performing in all those shows and living that life it didn't seem like real life at all. The acting bug has caught me big time. It was six months of total fantasy, during which anyone could be whoever they wanted to be and act in any way they wished. I suppose that is what being an actor is all about and, during my brief stint as an actor, I'm glad I at least learned that. If it had been real it wouldn't have been anywhere near as much fun.

22

FOR A STAND-UP COMEDIAN it's all about getting to play the Hammersmith Apollo. You've seen it on telly; you've seen the billboards of your comedy heroes outside; and you daydream of one day walking on that stage. When I was a kid I'd walk to school under the Hammersmith flyover and gaze up at the huge eight-storey tall awnings that hung along the outside and wonder just what Gloria Gaynor, The Police, Blondie or even Gary Numan sounded like live on that stage.

An androgynous, make-up wearing man who rarely smiled and quite clearly could not dance, Gary Numan was not a name you'd associate with black youths. The only reason he came into my consciousness was because Albert was a massive fan and I had to endure many nights of him playing the album *The Pleasure Principle* at 120 decibels until the early hours. Albert may have sailed through school and always had a new car or a new girlfriend but his taste in music was awful. Although looking back Gary Numan was indeed cool, as he ended up being a massive influence on American hip-hop stars Sir Mix-A-Lot (of 'Big Butts' fame), Puff Daddy and Kool G Rap. But I just didn't get it.

I've always thought that coolness is a bit overrated anyway.

Being cool isn't funny and even as a young kid I knew I had funny bones – well, people would often point and laugh at me, but that was probably because Mum would dress me and Stella in the same outfits. Cool guys smoke cigarettes and scowl a lot; that's not for me. Funny guys get the girls (and boys).

So when I first played the Apollo in 2007 it was like a dream come true. I never imagined, looking back at my days at Big Fish comedy, that I'd get to play the Hammersmith Apollo. I'd performed there before on gang shows with other comics, but this was my solo show. I'd managed to sell the place out (twice back to back!), so the champagne was going to be uncorked tonight. It's normal for me to feel nervous before a big gig, but that day I was nervous as hell walking through the empty auditorium. It was buzzing with the kind of technical activity that always precedes a show and lots of big guys called Dave were rushing about carrying bundles of cables and looking seriously underdressed. Technicians like nothing more than hanging around in empty posh theatres eating chips and looking like they've just rolled out of bed. There is, in fact, something magical about an empty auditorium before a big show. It's a bit like the feeling you get before a big storm breaks. There's electricity in the air. I felt the hairs on my forearms standing up on end and a static crackling by the sound desk. Was it anticipation? Or a faulty connection? I'd have to ask one of the Daves about it.

Stage fright is a funny thing. When I first started out in comedy I'd get it really badly. Experience has taught me never to eat less than three hours before any show. Let's just say your body has a strange way of dealing with stress and we'll leave it at that. It's good to be nervous because you can use that energy. You can get behind it and push it into excitement and enthusiasm. Sometimes you can push the gig right into orbit and it'll take hours to come down from the natural high – for me and hopefully for the audience. Adrenalin is like a drug and, once you've had it, you're hooked. Live stand-up comedy can be an amazing experience and if you don't believe me head down the London Comedy Store some time and see for yourself.

What I felt that day was not normal stage fright, however. It was pure fright. I'd just been told that I was having a couple of serious VIPs in the audience that night. My mum and dad were flying in from Nigeria to watch me perform. Once all the kids had grown up and moved out they'd gone home to Abeokuta to build a house and retire in peace. They keep saying they're building it for all of us kids, but I happen to know that Auntie Yomi, who went on to have a big family of her own, is living there. I've been there to visit them once and, if anything, they're trying to out-do Mama Ola's bathroom fetish, except, because of Auntie Yomi, they have a permanent *gbedu* (sound system) hooked up to a generator in the garden. But of course Mum refuses to use the generator because of all the locals who will turn up with their mobile phones looking to charge them up.

But now they were heading to the Hammersmith Apollo straight from the airport. Damn! What do I do? Most of my show is based on their funny antics. Do I now re-edit? What about sex gags? What about swearing? I never swear in front of my parents! A grown man, I was taken back to being a child again.

Yet more stressful was the fact that I remembered how my parents were not supportive of my initial forays into stand-up comedy. Now of course I realize that in their eyes English comedy meant *The Black and White Minstrel Show* and they were only looking out for me. At the time I perceived their lack of support to be discouraging. I remember my dad had never been happier than when I worked for the council, and when I quit he would keep bringing me application forms for the other 'jobs for life' and dropping subtle hints like 'When are you going to get a proper job?' or worse still 'Comedy? What is comedy? Are you a clown?'

It's not that they didn't get comedy or didn't understand jokes. It's just that in the seventies there were no comedians on TV that they could relate to. Coupled with Mum and Dad's harsh experiences, that kind of comedy just didn't speak to them. They spoke *about* them, using such words as 'nig-nog' or 'sambo'. In all my childhood years the only production they ever went to see at the theatre was the hit South African musical *Ipi Tombi*. Although they never took us kids, they went to see it twice and my parents aren't even from South Africa and they don't know any South African people. They just liked the idea of seeing black people on stage being played by black people and not by white people blacked up. So the notion of them spending good money to go and see any live theatrical event was pretty much alien to them.

Dad: 'Why go, spend money, sit down and keep quiet?'

Mum: 'And why eat in a restaurant when there is perfectly good food in the fridge at home?'

Now they were coming to the Hammersmith Apollo to watch me do my turn on the stage. So to say that I was bricking it would be an understatement.

For the show I had decided to open with a big musical number and a choreographed dance routine. It was meant to be a parody of Beyoncé's worldwide hit 'Put a Ring On It'. If you know the song and have seen the video you know it's a very sexy and suggestive routine when Beyoncé does it. When I do it, it only suggests that I can't dance. I'd even tried to master the very dodgy splits manoeuvre in the middle. Conservative Nigerian parents don't go in much for the splits. So I was running around backstage wringing my hands as the audience started arriving, hoping that

Mum and Dad would make it, but also kind of worried that they might.

We had fifteen professional dancers limbering up backstage to join me for the Beyoncé number. If you're stressing out about doing a big show and the imminent arrival of your disapproving parents then fifteen lithe young bodies in skintight spandex warming up in the wings can be a little bit . . . distracting. By the way, if you want to have a *really* good after-show party, then make sure to invite fifteen professionally trained dancers to come along – you won't regret it. It gets things off to a flying start.

Timekeeping has never been a problem for Mum and Dad, what with juggling multiple jobs and kids. The same can't be said of Nigerian Airways, who they were flying with. I was praying that the plane would take off in the region of on time and would land relatively near Heathrow Airport. I remembered the West African Airways flight we'd taken back when I was eleven with dread and the jokes that my sister and I had made about it years later. I'd do an impression of the stewardess: 'Welcome to West African Airways, or WAA, as you will soon be calling it. Your captain today is Ikeme Funa, an experienced fisherman and amateur pilot. If you are looking for the parachute under your seat, there is no parachute under your seat. Please use the lifejacket. In the case of emergency, if you see me screaming and running, follow! Leave everything and run!' I hoped that the Nigerian Airways flight would be wonderful. Not only did they have to land without incident but they had to get through baggage reclaim and customs. Like many people of the older generation, the concept of travelling light is a foreign one. I fully expected them to turn up at the theatre with a dozen huge trunks wrapped in cellophane as usual.

The other person who would be on-stage that day was my support act, Seann Walsh. Seann was looking very pale. Very pale indeed. So pale in fact that I was worried that under the bright lights of the stage his face would blind the front four rows. But looking at him, I thought, if he can handle the pressure then so can I goddamn it! Seann's a great comic, but he was still in his twenties at the time, drifting along at that magical age when you're living alone for the first time. Most people choose a house share but he'd gone for a canal boat anchored on the Thames just off Rotherhithe docks. They say adversity breeds comedy and he was having a lot of adversity at the time, trying to figure out how to install electricity and empty the chemical toilet. For some reason the girls absolutely loved him for all this. Young people! That's something that I'll never understand.

The other stalwart of the show was Nigel, my tour producer: totally stoic even in the most distressing of circumstances. He is probably so unflappable because he has poor eyesight. If you can't see the danger coming then you don't worry about it and so Nigel is very calm under pressure. He also has an outrageously beautiful female assistant, which makes me question just how blind he is. As far as I can tell, her main role is to answer his important questions like 'Oi! Where's Amos?' or 'Oi! Where's the stage?' She's very popular among the other comics as she mixes beauty with great disdain for all men: think Marlene Dietrich meets Grace Jones with the caustic wit of Bette Davis.

For this night, I had invested in a great new suit. I didn't ask Nigel his opinion. There's something to be said about feeling comfortable in what you're wearing that gives you an air of confidence. You know how some people say they have bad dreams about going back to school without any clothes on? Well, my nightmare is turning up on stage in front of a packed auditorium wearing last season's Vivienne Westwood. As *if* I would ever do that! (Please don't Google any of my fliers pre-2006. Let's just say I had a thing about bright colours and big lapels.)

One of my rituals as a stand-up comedian is standing backstage, listening to the excited murmur of the audience. Their voices are a bit like the instruments in an orchestra and in a few moments I would be taking up the conductor's baton. You always know it's going to be a good show when you can hear them whooping even before the show has started. Tuning their voices. It's hard to describe but the buzz created makes the room come alive. It reminds me about a 'true' story I heard about Haile Selassie, the great Ethiopian leader. He went to see an opera in London and at the end his friend asked him what he thought of the performance. He said he liked it very much but his favourite bit was at the start before the music really began and when all the instruments tune up together. It's the same for me in comedy with the audience chatter just before the start of the show.

At one minute to show-time we got our beginner's call. I peeped out from behind the wings and watched as the art deco interior and red velvet curtain, flaming under the stage lights, dimmed as we faded to blackout. The thudding base line kicked in. An anticipatory hush seized the crowd. The curtains parted and fifteen confident bodies swarmed the stage. I could hear the audience howling. I made my entrance.

Each and every one of those dancers were working their arses off. Thank God when I joined them I was in time. I threw in a couple of funny moves and the crowd went ballistic. The tenor reached fever pitch and I got goosebumps. The feeling was incredible. Then bam! The routine ended. The roar of the crowd was deafening. We'd caught them by surprise and we'd nailed it. As the lights changed to focus on me, I thanked my dancers and, looking down into the auditorium there, leading the applause, were my mum and dad, smiling from ear to ear.

The next hour and a half was surreal. I was so in the moment and the audience were with me all the way. There was absolutely no way I was going to throw this gig. The words were rolling out of my mouth and the laughter was coming back to me. The audience was participating with their minds, bodies, voices. It was just one of those magical nights when I could do no wrong.

A crescendo hit and, two encores later, I was exhausted. I was humbled by the reaction of the audience and my parents were there to see it. Yes! No council application forms tonight. I was so moved that I had to tell the audience that my mum and dad were there in the front row and it was the first time they'd seen me perform in ten years. The crowd went wild – applauding, whistling. My mum got up, turned around, and took a fucking bow – waving like the Queen. To date, it was the best show of my life.

Later, in the after-show bar, Mum and Dad were looking at the dancers with quizzical expressions. I went up to my dad and gave him a big hug and he returned it.

'Dad. You made it!'

'Son, we wouldn't miss it for the world.'

'What did you think?

'It was amazing! The dancers! The music! And all those people.'

'I'm glad you liked it.'

'We always knew you'd do well.'

'Really? So you approve now?'

'Son, you don't need our approval. The lizard that jumped from the high iroko tree and landed safely said he would praise himself if no one else did. You have already proven everything you need to prove. And remember the iroko tree is pretty high, but I like the Hammersmith Apollo better.'

He sipped his Guinness and then said with a smile, 'Because the fruits of it are sweeter. Another round for my son!'